FOR UNTO US

40 Prophetic Insights about Jesus,
Justice, and Gentiles from the
Prophet Isaiah

PETER DEHAAN

For Unto Us: 40 Prophetic Insights about Jesus, Justice, and Gentiles from the Prophet Isaiah Copyright © 2020, 2022 by Peter DeHaan.

Book 3 in the Dear Theophilus series.

Second edition. (First published as *Dear Theophilus, Isaiah: 40 Prophetic Insights about Jesus, Justice, and Gentiles*)

All rights reserved: No part of this book may be reproduced, disseminated, or transmitted in any form, by any means, or for any purpose without the express written consent of the author or his legal representatives. The only exceptions are short excerpts, and the cover image, for reviews or academic research. For permissions: peterdehaan.com/contact.

Scripture quotations taken from The Holy Bible, New International Version® NIV® Copyright © 1973 1978 1984 2011 by Biblica, Inc.™ Used by permission. All rights reserved worldwide.

ISBN:
    978-1-948082-82-2 (e-book)
    978-1-948082-83-9 (paperback)
    978-1-948082-84-6 (hardcover)

Library of Congress Control Number: 2021923777

Published by Rock Rooster Books, Grand Rapids, Michigan

Credits:
    Developmental editor: Erin Brown
    Copy editor/proofreader: Robyn Mulder
    Cover design: Taryn Nergaard
    Author photo: Chelsie Jensen Photography

To Jonathan Alexander

Books in the Dear Theophilus series

That You May Know: A 40-Day Devotional Exploring the Life of Jesus from the Gospel of Luke

Tongues of Fire: 40 Devotional Insights for Today's Church from the Book of Acts

For Unto Us: 40 Prophetic Insights about Jesus, Justice, and Gentiles from the Prophet Isaiah

Return to Me: 40 Prophetic Teachings about Unfaithfulness, Punishment, and Hope from the Minor Prophets

I Hope in Him: 40 Insights about Moving from Despair to Deliverance through the Life of Job

Living Water: 40 Reflections on Jesus's Life and Love from the Gospel of John

PETER DEHAAN

Love Is Patient: 40 Devotional Gems and Bible Study Truths from Paul's Letters to the Corinthians

A New Heaven and a New Earth: 40 Practical Insights from John's Book of Revelation

Be the first to hear about Peter's new books and receive updates at PeterDeHaan.com/updates.

Contents

Who Is Isaiah?...1

Day 1: Wrong Worship 5

Day 2: The Branch of the Lord........................9

Day 3: Send Me.. 13

    Dig Deeper: Holy, Holy, Holy...................... 17

Day 4: A Sign.. 19

    Dig Deeper: Isaiah's Boys 23

Day 5: A Child Is Born 25

Day 6: Injustice 29

    Dig Deeper: Woe 33

Day 7: Harmony among God's Creatures.... 37

Day 8: Isaiah's Psalm of Praise 41

    Dig Deeper: Four Kings of Judah............... 45

Day 9: The Arrogant Will Fall........................ 49

Day 10: The Pride of Moab 53

   Dig Deeper: Judge with Justice 57

Day 11: Refocus on What Matters 59

Day 12: An Astounding Turnaround 63

Day 13: Water for the Thirsty 67

Day 14: Eat, Drink, and Be Merry 71

   Dig Deeper: Isaiah in the New Testament . 75

Day 15: Seventy Years 79

Day 16: The End Times 83

   Dig Deeper: The Ethiopian Treasurer
   Reads Isaiah 87

Day 17: My Holy Mountain 89

Day 18: The Desire of Our Hearts 93

Day 19: Going Home 97

   Dig Deeper: The Leviathan 101

Day 20: A Precious Cornerstone 103

Day 21: Going through the Motions 107

   Dig Deeper: The Potter and the Clay 111

Day 22: Lie to Us 113

Day 23: Who Is Our Lord? 117

- Dig Deeper: Other Nations 121
- Day 24: A Future Healing 125
- Day 25: Where's Your Confidence? 129
  - Dig Deeper: A Historical Account 133
- Day 26: Prayer Makes a Difference 135
- Day 27: Don't Show Off 139
  - Dig Deeper: Gentiles 143
- Day 28: Jesus and Justice 145
  - Dig Deeper: Names Matter 149
- Day 29: I Am 151
  - Dig Deeper: There Is No Other 155
- Day 30: Fate or Freedom? 157
  - Dig Deeper: Who Is Bel? 161
- Day 31: Our Mentor 163
  - Dig Deeper: Peace Like a River 167
- Day 32: A Light to the World 169
- Day 33: Bring Good News 173
  - Dig Deeper: The Arm of the Lord 177
- Day 34: Sing and Rejoice 179
- Day 35: Seek God 183

Day 36: Fasting, Failure, and Fisticuffs 187

Day 37: No More Sun 191

    Dig Deeper: The Armor of God 195

Day 38: Be Like Jesus 197

Day 39: Do Not Grieve the Holy Spirit 201

    Dig Deeper: The New Heaven and the
    New Earth 205

Day 40: Answer the Call 209

For Small Groups, Sunday Schools,
and Classrooms 213

Bonus Content: If You're New to the Bible 215

Acknowledgments 219

About the Dear Theophilus Series 221

About Peter DeHaan 223

Books by Peter DeHaan 225

Who Is Isaiah?

Isaiah is a prophet in the Old Testament of the Bible. He is called a major prophet, along with Jeremiah, Ezekiel, and Daniel. This classification doesn't mean they're more important than the twelve minor prophets. This designation is because their books are much longer than those of the minor prophets. In fact, at sixty-six chapters, the book of Isaiah is the second-longest book in the Bible, trailing only Psalms with its 150 chapters.

Isaiah's dad is Amoz. The Bible tells us nothing about Amoz other than he is Isaiah's father, which it does often. Isaiah's public career as a prophet spans several decades, during the reigns of four kings of Judah: Uzziah, Jotham, Ahaz, and Hezekiah. Isaiah is a contemporary of the prophets Amos, Hosea, and Micah.

During Isaiah's ministry, Assyria conquered Israel (sometimes called the Northern Kingdom) and relocated the people. Judah (sometimes referred to as the Southern Kingdom) is all that remains of God's people. Babylon will later conquer them. Isaiah warns the people about this, but the conquest doesn't happen during his ministry.

Many of Isaiah's prophecies consider God's people in the near term, but other prophecies look forward several centuries to the coming of Jesus, as well as John the Baptist, who precedes Jesus. The New Testament quotes many of Isaiah's words, making him a favorite prophet of many people.

There are two notable occurrences. First, when Jesus reads Scripture in the synagogue, he reads a passage from Isaiah, which prophetically looks forward to the coming Savior. Then Jesus proclaims himself as the fulfillment of that passage. How bold and unexpected—and fully appropriate.

Another notable New Testament story is the Ethiopian eunuch. As he reads from the book of Isaiah, Philip approaches him and explains the meaning of Isaiah's prophecy about Jesus. The Ethiopian man believes in Jesus, and Philip baptizes him.

Even centuries after Isaiah died, his words still influenced others, just as they can influence us today.

While we may not have the influence of Isaiah, what can we do to influence people during our lifetime and even after we're gone?

[Discover more about Isaiah in 2 Kings 19–20, John 1:23, Luke 3:4, Matthew 8:17, Luke 4:16–21, and Acts 8:26–39.]

Day 1:

Wrong Worship

Isaiah 1–2

Stop bringing meaningless offerings! Your incense is detestable to me. New Moons, Sabbaths and convocations—I cannot bear your worthless assemblies. Isaiah 1:13

In addition to giving the people a bunch of rules—things they should and shouldn't do—the Old Testament teaches two primary ways to worship God. One is through sacrifices, and the other is by a series of annual celebrations and festivals. Both forms of worship stand at the center of Jewish religion, and the Hebrew society revolves around these practices.

Yet God is not pleased with their worship. The book of Isaiah starts by recording God's words of criticism for his people's religious practices, calling their offerings meaningless. He takes no pleasure in what they give.

Why? Because the people offer their sacrifices with bad attitudes and wrong perspectives. Their approach to God is off. Their sacrifices don't honor him. Instead, they dishonor him.

What God intended as a way to connect his people with him has the opposite effect. It drives a wedge between him and them. And they don't realize it. They're going through the motions, but as far as God is concerned, it's meaningless activity.

Then God launches into criticism of their various celebrations. He goes as far as to say that he hates their practices. The way his people approach these festivals burdens God and wearies him. Because of their wrong approach, he has even stopped considering their prayers. He closes his eyes when they lift their hands in prayer and doesn't listen to their words. All of this is because their worship is off base.

What does God want instead?

He doesn't ask for sacrifices or seek a better observance of the religious holidays he mandated. Instead, he wants practical action. He tells them to wash up and get spiritually clean. They must stop wronging other people and pursuing evil that disgraces God. Rather, he wants them to do right. This includes to seek justice, defend the oppressed, and help widows and orphans.

God's criticism of his people's worship comes out as a harsh rebuke.

I wonder how he views our worship today. Does he regard our offerings as meaningless and our assemblies—our church services and religious holidays—as worthless? I want to say no, but I fear the answer is yes. God forgive us. May we do better.

Do we approach God with the right attitude? Is he pleased with our worship or irritated by it?

[Discover more about worshiping God in Matthew 4:10, Mark 7:7, John 4:23–24, and Romans 12:1.]

Day 2:

The Branch of the Lord

Isaiah 3–4

In that day the Branch of the Lord will be beautiful and glorious, and the fruit of the land will be the pride and glory of the survivors in Israel. Isaiah 4:2

Isaiah looks forward to the day when the Branch of the Lord will appear. Branch, with a capital *B*, is a euphemism for Jesus, who will come to rescue God's people. Isaiah says this Branch will emerge as awesome and full of wonder, which is an understatement considering all that Jesus did, is doing, and will do. Jesus will produce fruit for the people. They will take pride in what the Branch produces and glory in it.

Jesus, the Branch—our Branch—will come for us, spiritually feeding us with his fruit: beautiful, wondrous fruit, the source of pride and glory.

Just as Jesus is *the* Branch, we are *his* branches, that's branches with a lowercase *b*. We are branches connected to the Branch (which John calls the "true vine"). But being a branch connected to *the* Branch isn't enough. Having a mere connection with Jesus is insufficient. When we're connected with the Branch of Jesus, we must bear fruit. And we must produce good fruit. That's what Father God, our Papa, expects from us.

If we produce no fruit, God, our gardener, will cut off our branch. Yikes! He'll lop us off. We're not worthy of remaining connected to Jesus if we produce no fruit—if we accomplish nothing for him. That's a sobering truth. Having a connection with Jesus isn't enough if it produces nothing. We can't pledge our allegiance to him and then coast through life unchanged. He expects us to produce fruit because of our connection to him.

To further the analogy, every branch that produces fruit will eventually face pruning. This isn't punishment. Instead, it's a beneficial process that will allow us to produce even more fruit. While an untrimmed tree will yield some fruit, a tree pruned properly will produce much more. God, our gardener, will prune us so that we can make even more fruit for him.

But to do this we must remain with God, connected to Jesus, and bearing fruit. Else we risk him cutting off our branch, throwing us into the fire, and having the flames consume us.

Are we producing fruit through Jesus and for Jesus? Are we willing to let God prune us so we can produce even more?

[Discover more about Jesus as the Branch in Isaiah 11:1, Jeremiah 23:5, Jeremiah 33:15, Zechariah 3:8, and Zechariah 6:12. Discover more about us as branches in John 15:1–6.]

Day 3:

Send Me

Isaiah 5–6

Then I heard the voice of the Lord saying, "Whom shall I send? And who will go for us?" And I said, "Here am I. Send me!" Isaiah 6:8

Isaiah has a vision. He sees into heaven where God sits exalted on his throne. It's grand, glorious. His flowing robe fills the temple. Seraphim—heavenly beings with six wings—fly above God in continuous worship of their Creator. They sing, "Holy, holy, holy." This is not a gentle, reverent chant. Instead, it's bold, thunderous, echoing. Their voices shake the temple. It fills with smoke.

God's glory overwhelms Isaiah. "Woe is me," he groans. He recognizes his mistakes, his sins, his words spoken in error. Full of guilt, he trembles in fear before a perfect God. Isaiah feels ruined by his shortcomings.

But God doesn't leave Isaiah quaking in his unworthiness. Instead, an angel symbolically purifies Isaiah's lips, taking away his guilt and redressing his mistakes. Isaiah is ready, now poised to speak before holy God.

But before Isaiah can say a word, God speaks. "Who can I send? Who will go as our messenger?"

It's not that God doesn't have anyone to send. It's that he hopes Isaiah will volunteer.

Isaiah does. As if raising his hand, jumping up and down, Isaiah shouts, "Send me, God! Please, send me!" It's like, with the game on the line, Isaiah says, "Put me in, Coach. I can do it!"

That's exactly what God wanted. Then God gives Isaiah a message for the people. It's a difficult one—a warning about hearing but not understanding, about seeing but not perceiving, about the hard hearts of a calloused people who don't comprehend God's ways. But if they can hear and see and understand, then they can turn to God and receive his healing.

It's a message for the people then, and a message for us today: turn to God and receive healing.

Just as Isaiah says, "Send me," Jesus says, "I'm here, Dad, ready to do your will." Jesus comes to earth to be the ultimate sacrifice and redress the things we do wrong. He dies and then overcomes death so that we can live again. Jesus is why we can turn to God and receive healing.

Thank you, Jesus, for saying yes to Papa.

Are we ready to do what God asks us to do?

[Discover more about Jesus's willing sacrifice in Hebrews 10:5–7 and Psalm 40:6–8.]

Dig Deeper:

Holy, Holy, Holy

And they were calling to one another: "Holy, holy, holy is the Lord Almighty; the whole earth is full of his glory." Isaiah 6:3

In Isaiah's grand vision, he sees seraphim worshiping God in heaven. They fly above him, whooping, "Holy, holy, holy is the Lord God Almighty. Earth is full of your glory."

Does this sound familiar?

In another vision, this one in the New Testament, John also has a supernatural encounter. It's an epic revelation. John also sees into heaven. Four living creatures with six wings worship God continuously. They also proclaim that God is "Holy, holy, holy." Then they confirm his eternal nature as being past, present, and future.

These are the only two instances in the Bible that the word *holy* repeats three times. Why three? For emphasis. Affirming God as holy stands as a true statement. Saying that he is holy, holy doubles the impact. But to make sure we don't miss the point, Isaiah's and John's visions emphasize God's holiness threefold. That way we won't overlook it.

Holy is the only word that's repeated three times in succession in the Bible. It's a reference to God's nature. May we never forget to worship God as our holy, holy, holy, glorious, eternal, and almighty God.

What does it mean to us to have a God who is holy, holy, holy?

[Discover more about worshiping God as holy in Psalm 99:9, Romans 12:1, Revelation 4:8, and Revelation 15:4.]

Day 4:

A Sign

Isaiah 7–8

Again the Lord spoke to Ahaz, "Ask the Lord your God for a sign, whether in the deepest depths or in the highest heights." But Ahaz said, "I will not ask; I will not put the Lord to the test." Isaiah 7:10–12

God speaks to King Ahaz through Isaiah: "Ask me for a sign, anything. Nothing is too hard or too grand."

But Ahaz refuses. "I will not ask for a sign," he says. "I will not test God."

Did Ahaz answer wisely or foolishly?

Other people in the Bible sought a sign from God. When Gideon asks, once is not enough. He does it twice in a row. God promised to save Israel through Gideon. But Gideon doubts God and asks for a sign by laying a piece of wool on the ground. He tells God that if dew is on the fleece in the morning but not on the ground, then Gideon will believe God's promise. God answers by drenching the wool and leaving the ground dry.

I don't know if Gideon still doubts or if he doesn't like the answer, but he asks God for a second sign. This time he requests the opposite outcome. His request is that God is to put dew on the ground but not the fleece. God does as Gideon requested. A double confirmation. Case closed.

Another time, King Hezekiah is sick. Isaiah (yep, the prophet Isaiah, the one this book is about) goes to him and tells him to put his affairs in order, for he's going to die. Hezekiah prays to God in earnest despair. God hears the king's petition and relents. As a sign of confirmation, Hezekiah asks God to make the shadow of the sun move backward. God does, and Hezekiah lives another fifteen years.

Yet Jesus, when tempted by Satan, refuses to put God to the test. This aligns with the command in Deuteronomy to not put God to the test.

Back to our question about Ahaz. Did he answer wisely or foolishly by refusing to ask God for a sign? We don't know. God neither commends nor condemns Ahaz for refusing to ask for a sign. Nonetheless, God gives him one. It's a prophetic sign, one of the most popular ones in the Bible.

What is this sign? It's both simple and outrageous. It will bring into reality the singular, most important event in all history: A virgin will get pregnant and give birth to a baby boy. We call him Immanuel, which means "God with us."

Have we ever asked God for a sign? Was this a good idea?

[Discover more about signs from God and putting him to the test in Judges 6:36–40, 2 Kings 20:1–11, and Isaiah 38:1–8, as well as Deuteronomy 6:16 and Luke 4:12.]

Day 5:

A Child Is Born

Isaiah 9

For to us a child is born, to us a son is given, and the government will be on his shoulders. And he will be called Wonderful Counselor, Mighty God, Everlasting Father, Prince of Peace. Isaiah 9:6

The book of Isaiah contains many prophecies that look forward to Jesus, the people's promised and much-anticipated coming King. In what may be the best known of these prophecies, Isaiah gives us amazing and comforting characteristics about our future Savior, Jesus.

Isaiah starts by saying that Jesus will come as a child, God's gift to us. Father God will send Jesus to us as an infant, who will grow up to become our supreme ruler for the rest of time.

Though Isaiah doesn't specifically call him *Jesus*, the prophet does give us four other awesome names.

First, we'll call him *Wonderful Counselor*. Though anyone can give advice, not all advice is good, and some is even bad. Not so with Jesus. His words will come forth as instruction of a most amazing nature, possessing a distinguished authority.

Mighty God emerges as a second title for Jesus. Yes, Jesus is God. Beyond being godlike, Jesus will possess all of God's characteristics, including being almighty.

Jesus's third title builds upon his second one: *Everlasting Father*. This is a bit confusing because if Jesus is God's Son, how can he also be the Father? But remember that Jesus and the Father are one. What we see in one, we see in the other. However, let's focus on the word *everlasting*. Jesus is eternal, transcending all time. He participated in creation, and we will celebrate him in the new heaven and new earth, which is to come.

The fourth name for Jesus is *Prince of Peace*. He will usher in an era of perpetual harmony, ruling with excellence for the rest of time.

Last, this child—Jesus, whom God will send—will grow up to rule us. As a descendant of King David, Jesus's government will have no end, for it will extend into eternity. And, unlike human rulers with their frailties, Jesus will oversee his people with perfect, flawless justice.

Jesus is more than our Savior. He is our eternal King, who will usher in peace and rule with perfect justice for all time without end.

Do we stand in astonished awe of who Jesus is and what he has accomplished and will accomplish?

[Discover more about Jesus's characteristics in Luke 4:32, John 1:1–3, John 14:9, John 17:21, Revelation 21:23, and Revelation 22:16.]

Day 6:

Injustice

Isaiah 10

Woe to those who make unjust laws, to those who issue oppressive decrees, to deprive the poor of their rights and withhold justice from the oppressed of my people, making widows their prey and robbing the fatherless.
Isaiah 10:1–2

Isaiah directs one of his woes at people who pursue injustice. To make sure we don't skim past this, he gives several examples. People who engage in these activities deserve woe: profound misfortune.

The first part of this warning is to those who make unjust laws. It refers to people in power who legislate rules that favor one group over others—often themselves and their kind—at the expense of those in different situations or who hold opposing views. History is replete with unjust laws. It's easy for us in the present to look at the past and shake our heads, dismayed over the biased nature of these laws. But it's a little harder to spot unjust laws in the present, especially if we helped enact them or they benefit us.

Parallel to people making unjust laws are those who issue oppressive decrees. This can come from two sources. One group is bureaucrats charged with interpreting, implementing, and enacting laws made by others. They can make prejudiced interpretations. The other group includes judges who decide if a person has broken the law. Injustice occurs when judges interpret the law through the lens of their own biases. If they have an agenda, they risk rendering prejudicial judgments.

The third form of injustice comes from those who deprive poor people of what they rightfully deserve. In this case, it isn't unfair laws or oppressive interpretations. Instead, it denies people what they legally deserve. We see this in unequal enforcement or the subjective prosecution of existing laws.

Next, injustice occurs when people take advantage of those who lack the ability or resources to defend themselves. In biblical times, widows were a prime target of the unscrupulous rich who exploited them for financial gain.

Following closely with the idea of preying on widows is stealing from orphans. The fatherless have no voice and few advocates—aside from God and his prophets—in Bible times. The situation isn't all that different today. And we can interpret this to include any disadvantaged or marginalized people or groups.

Woe to these people who pursue injustice. Joy to those who promote justice, for the pursuit of justice is a worthy, God-honoring practice.

What can we do to pursue justice? How can we act justly in all we do?

[Discover more about pursuing justice in Exodus 23:6, Deuteronomy 16:19, 1 Kings 10:9, Ezra 7:25, Matthew 12:18–21, and Revelation 19:11.]

Dig Deeper:

Woe

"Woe to me!" I cried. "I am ruined! For I am a man of unclean lips, and I live among a people of unclean lips, and my eyes have seen the King, the Lord Almighty." Isaiah 6:5

The word *woe* occurs twenty-three times in Isaiah, far more than in any other book in the Bible. Woe is a small word with a big meaning. It portends sorrow, grief, and misery.

Six of these warnings of woe occur in chapter 5. And once Isaiah even says, "Woe is me" when he realizes just how inadequate he is in God's awesome, overwhelming presence.

Here are some of the warnings of woe in the book of Isaiah:

- Woe to a sinful nation (Isaiah 1:4).

- Woe to those who boast in their sin (Isaiah 3:9).
- Woe to the wicked (Isaiah 3:11).
- Woe to those who develop all the land, leaving nowhere for people to live (Isaiah 5:8).
- Woe to those who spend their time drinking (Isaiah 5:11).
- Woe to those who persist in their sin (Isaiah 5:18).
- Woe to those who call evil good and good evil (Isaiah 5:20).
- Woe to those who think they're wise (Isaiah 5:21).
- Woe to those who drink in excess (Isaiah 5:22).
- Woe to those who pervert justice (Isaiah 10:1).
- Woe to nations that rage and peoples who roar (Isaiah 17:12).
- Woe to those who let wine overcome them (Isaiah 28:1).
- Woe to those who think they can hide from God (Isaiah 29:15).

- Woe to obstinate children—and people (Isaiah 30:1).
- Woe to those who trust others to save them (Isaiah 31:1).
- Woe to those who fight their Creator (Isaiah 45:9).
- Woe to those who disrespect their parents (Isaiah 45:10).

Many of Isaiah's other warnings of woe are to specific people and places.

What do we need to change in our lives to avoid Isaiah's warnings of woe?

[Discover more about woe in Matthew 23:15–16, Matthew 26:24, Mark 14:21, Luke 6:24–26, Luke 17:1, 1 Corinthians 9:16, and Jude 1:11.]

Day 7:

Harmony among God's Creatures

Isaiah 11

The wolf will live with the lamb, the leopard will lie down with the goat, the calf and the lion and the yearling together; and a little child will lead them. Isaiah 11:6

As Isaiah continues his discourse, he shares an interesting view of the future. In this serene vision of what is to come, animals will live in harmony with one another and at peace with people. It's idyllic. It's ideal. And it may be what God intended all along when he created us and our world.

To demonstrate this peace in the animal kingdom, Isaiah pairs unlikely beasts in a series of contrasts that show a different reality for what is to come.

He says that wolves and lambs will peacefully coexist. That leopards will sleep next to goats. And that calves and lions will eat their food together. Not only will these carnivores not eat other animals in the food chain but, also, children will lead them. Imagine that: a little child guiding wolves, leopards, and lions in a peaceful procession of the animal kingdom—not tamed beasts but creatures restored to their rightful function as God created them.

Animals will neither harm one another nor fear or attack humans. In this, we'll witness—and experience—harmony in God's creation.

Furthermore, cows and bears will eat alongside one another. Their babies will nap together. As a bonus, lions will munch on plants instead of other creatures. It could be that this future reality will have no carnivores, where people and animals will subsist on produce and not each other.

Since Adam and Eve were vegetarians, and humans didn't eat meat until after the flood, we can argue that the same may have held true for animals. If so, Isaiah's tranquil vision for the future alludes to the purity and perfection of God's original creation.

But there's more. And it's shocking. A baby will safely play where cobras live, even reaching into a nest of vipers without suffering a fatal bite.

In the future, on God's holy mountain, animals and people won't hurt each other. They will not kill. They'll live in harmony, full of peace—just as they did in the beginning.

What can we do today to move toward this future harmony that God promises?

[Discover more about the behavior of God's animals in Genesis 3:14–15, Genesis 9:1–3, Numbers 22:28–30, Isaiah 65:25, and Acts 28:3–5.]

Day 8:

Isaiah's Psalm of Praise

Isaiah 12

Surely God is my salvation; I will trust and not be afraid. The Lord, the Lord himself, is my strength and my defense; he has become my salvation. Isaiah 12:2

The book of Psalms contains 150 hymns from the Hebrew culture. It includes both short and long ones. Some comfort and others confound with the dreadfulness of their content. Also, these sacred songs have a variety of themes.

Many of the psalms worship God, extolling his virtues, goodness, and largess. They celebrate who he is, what he did, and even what he will do. Other psalms flow as agonizing laments, bemoaning injustice or groaning about the writers' enemies. Some psalms read as a personal, heartfelt prayer journal that reveals the utter angst of their authors' souls.

Yet not all of the Bible's psalms are in the book of Psalms. We also find psalms scattered throughout the Old Testament. We encounter one of them today in Isaiah 12. And, depending on how we read the text, we might consider the passage as containing two short complementary psalms. Regardless, we can classify this passage as an uplifting song of worship and praise.

This hymn, however, isn't something Isaiah embraces as appropriate at that time or for the current state of the nation. Instead, he unveils this as a song that people will sing in the future, a future much different from their present. In that day they will praise God, who was once angry but now offers comfort. They will celebrate his name, telling everyone what he has done. They will sing and shout about the great Holy One.

The focus of their exultation is God's salvation. He will come and rescue them from their enemies, restore them as a nation, and reunite them as a people. Because of this, they will trust him and push aside fear. He will be strong for them and defend them from their foes. He will save them from their dire situation, which will fill them with joy, appreciation, and praise.

May we always remember to praise God for who he is, what he has done, and the things he will do. He is worthy of our admiration, and it's right for us to honor him because of it.

How can we best praise God?

[Discover more about praising God in Genesis 14:20, Deuteronomy 8:10, Judges 5:3, 1 Chronicles 16:25, Matthew 15:31, Luke 19:37, Romans 15:7–9, and 2 Corinthians 1:3.]

Dig Deeper:

Four Kings of Judah

I will establish your royal throne over Israel forever, as I promised David your father when I said, "You shall never fail to have a successor on the throne of Israel." 1 Kings 9:5

Isaiah's ministry spans the reigns of four kings of Judah: Uzziah, Jotham, Ahaz, and Hezekiah. King Uzziah reigns the longest. He's followed by his son Jotham. Jotham's son Ahaz succeeds him. Ahaz's son Hezekiah follows him.

It's a father, son, grandson, and great-grandson progression. They're all descendants of King David. Of these four kings, we know the most about King Hezekiah.

Here are the passages where Isaiah mentions these kings:

- Uzziah (Isaiah 1:1, Isaiah 6:1, and Isaiah 7:1)
- Jotham (Isaiah 1:1 and Isaiah 7:1)
- Ahaz (Isaiah 1:1, Isaiah 7:1–3, Isaiah 7:10–12, and Isaiah 14:28)
- Hezekiah (Isaiah 1:1 and Isaiah 36–39)

These four kings also appear in the historical text of 2 Kings and in the parallel historical book of 2 Chronicles. Some of these accounts overlap, while others provide complementary details.

- Uzziah, also called Azariah (2 Kings 15:1–7 and 2 Chronicles 26:1–27:2)
- Jotham (2 Kings 15:32–38, 2 Chronicles 26:21, and 2 Chronicles 27:1–9)
- Ahaz (2 Kings 16:1–20 and 2 Chronicles 27:9–28:27)
- Hezekiah (2 Kings 18–20 and 2 Chronicles 29–32)

The book of 2 Chronicles, which looks at history from a more spiritual perspective, declares that Uzziah did right in God's eyes and that Jotham walked steadfastly with God. However, Ahaz proved himself unfaithful to God. Last, Hezekiah did many positive things, but he had a moment of pride that displeased God.

What spiritual legacy will we leave for future generations?

[Discover more about the descendants of David and the family tree of Jesus in Matthew 1:6–16.]

Day 9:

The Arrogant Will Fall

Isaiah 13–14

You said in your heart, "I will ascend to the heavens; I will raise my throne above the stars of God"... But you are brought down to the realm of the dead, to the depths of the pit.
Isaiah 14:13–15

Some of Isaiah's prophecies are against the nation of Babylon, a growing powerhouse that will eventually conquer large parts of the region, including Judah. The book of Isaiah mentions Babylon eighteen times. This seems like a lot, but it's not as often as in Jeremiah, Ezekiel, and Daniel. The book of 2 Kings also frequently mentions Babylon.

Some of Isaiah's prophecies about Babylon state that it will conquer Judah. But even more so, Isaiah predicts Babylon's eventual fall. How this must comfort the nation of Judah, knowing that in the end, Babylon will get what it deserves for all the destruction it will cause. Today's passage anticipates that time.

Isaiah envisions the people's mockery of Babylon as well as their celebration of its downfall. In doing so, they'll rant about Babylon's arrogance. While desiring to make itself great, it tried to rival the greatness of God and, in fact, even presumed to become like him.

Like most arrogant people, despite having momentary success, Babylon will fail to hold on to what was once in its grasp. It will go down. Hard. The former great nation will enter the domain of the deceased. They will descend into the deep of the pit.

How Babylon's eventual downfall must encourage the people of Judah. But they miss that before Babylon faces its defeat, it will first conquer Judah and carry off most of the people into captivity. Isaiah prophesies that this will happen too.

Yes, the proud will fall. But this won't occur until after Babylon inflicts significant turmoil in the region. Just as they conquered others, another nation will conquer them. As the Bible says, a person (and a nation) reaps what he sows.

James warns about the folly of pursuing arrogant schemes, of boasting in what we plan to do. Planning by itself isn't bad, but scheming without factoring God's will into our plans is.

Instead of puffed-up boasting in what we will do under our own power, we are wise to place our confidence in God and condition our plans under the provision of his will.

Do our plans include God?

[Discover more about arrogance in Genesis 11:3–9, 1 Samuel 2:3, Nehemiah 9:29, Psalm 5:5, Psalm 31:18, 1 Timothy 6:17, and James 4:13–16, with more info in Galatians 6:7.]

Day 10:

The Pride of Moab

Isaiah 15–16

We have heard of Moab's pride—how great is her arrogance!—of her conceit, her pride and her insolence; but her boasts are empty. Therefore the Moabites wail, they wail together for Moab. Isaiah 16:6–7

Parallel with the arrogance of Babylon is the pride of Moab. Isaiah talks a lot about Moab, too, almost as much as he mentions Babylon.

The history of Moab is interesting. It goes back to Lot, Abraham's nephew. In one of the Bible's more sordid tales, Lot's daughters, desperate for children, get their father drunk and sleep with him. Yes, it's disgusting, but it's included in the Bible for us to see just how depraved we humans are. Yet God still loves us and uses us in his unfolding story. As a result of this incestuous encounter, Lot's oldest daughter gives birth to a son. She calls him Moab. He becomes the father of the Moabite nation.

Fast-forward to Moses leading God's people back into the Promised Land. They arrive at Moab's border, but they don't attack. Even so, the people of Moab quake at the number of people camped at the edge of their country. They become proactive, not militarily, but spiritually.

They hire Balaam to curse God's people. Balaam asserts that he can say only the words God gives him. The Moabites want his help anyway. Yet when Balaam opens his mouth, the people don't hear curses against Israel, but blessings. They give Balaam another chance and then a third. Each time he opens his mouth, he blesses Israel, making Moab's situation even worse.

Fortunately for Moab, God has already told Moses to leave Moab alone. "Don't harass them or provoke them," he says. "You are not to take their land."

This instruction, however, doesn't protect Moab forever. Isaiah launches into a lengthy prophecy against Moab. He talks about their reputation as a prideful nation, coupled with great arrogance. Additionally, Isaiah rails against Moab's conceit, insolence, and empty boasts.

Punishment for their pride will lead to their downfall. In the end, they will wail over what they have lost. As King Solomon said, pride does indeed precede destruction, with haughtiness coming before a fall.

What can we do to remove unwarranted pride from our lives?

[Discover more about pride in Proverbs 11:2, Proverbs 16:18, James 1:9–10, and 1 John 2:16. Learn more about Moab in Genesis 19:36–37, Numbers 22–24, Deuteronomy 2:9, and Isaiah 25:10.]

Dig Deeper:

Judge with Justice

In love a throne will be established; in faithfulness a man will sit on it—one from the house of David—one who in judging seeks justice and speeds the cause of righteousness.
Isaiah 16:5

Justice is a recurring theme in the book of Isaiah. The word occurs 130 times in the Bible, with thirty of them found in Isaiah. Many of these verses bemoan the absence of justice as well as the unjust actions of God's chosen people. But other passages command justice and anticipate a future liberation. (We've already covered "Injustice" on Day 6. And we will cover "Jesus and Justice" on Day 28.)

Isaiah begins by telling his people to do the right thing: seek justice and defend the oppressed. This includes helping orphans and widows. A few verses later he looks forward to the just liberation of his people.

God is just in all he does. And Jesus, a direct descendant of King David, will reign with justice and righteousness forever. In his rule, he will seek justice and advance right living. He will judge with integrity.

And this justice isn't just for the Jews. It's for the Gentiles too. It's for everyone.

How do we seek justice for everyone?

[Discover more about justice in Isaiah 1:17, Isaiah 1:27, Isaiah 5:22–23, Isaiah 9:7, Isaiah 28:6, Isaiah 28:17, Isaiah 29:20–21, Isaiah 30:18, Isaiah 32:1, Isaiah 42:1–4, Isaiah 51:5, Isaiah 59:15, and Isaiah 61:8.]

Day 11:

Refocus on What Matters

Isaiah 17–18

In that day people will look to their Maker and turn their eyes to the Holy One of Israel.
Isaiah 17:7

As Isaiah continues his prophecies of future events, he foresees a time when people will turn back to God, Israel's Holy One. They will return their attention to their Creator, the God who made them.

This refocusing on what matters means turning away from what they are wrongly giving their attention to. What does this include? Their religious practices, both those opposed by God and those he ordained, because they lost sight of the reason why. Together these serve to distract them from God, getting in the way of the relationship he wants to have with his people.

As they refocus on their Lord, on what matters most, they turn away from their altars. These manmade shrines distract them from their Creator. Yes, throughout time, God's people built altars to him, starting with Noah and then Abraham, followed by Isaac. Later, Moses built an altar to God. Then God specifically commanded Moses to make a special altar, providing detailed instructions for its exact construction. Still later, Joshua built an altar to God, too, as did Gideon and many others.

The people built these altars as monuments to honor God and worship him. Sometimes the people regarded these altars in a God-honoring way, but other times they missed the purpose of these memorials.

Of course, the Bible also tells us about altars to other gods, such as Baal. These altars existed in opposition to God. You'd think God's people would know they should avoid worshiping at altars to other gods, but they didn't. They lost sight of revering God and pursued other gods instead.

In addition to constructing altars to other gods, they also made Asherah poles, which they used in their worship of the goddess Asherah. This distracted God's people from their rightful worship of him.

In addition to altars and Asherah poles, a third spiritual distraction comes from incense altars. Even though God prescribed the use of incense in worshiping him, along with altars, he never paired the two together. God never told the people to build incense altars. Yet they did, with godly leaders often destroying these incense altars because they distracted the people from their worship of God.

When we encounter distractions in our lives, we move our focus from God. We shouldn't depend on increased self-discipline to maintain our attention on what is right. Instead, we should remove all distractions so we can best reorient our minds to what matters most: God.

Where do we place our focus?

[Discover more about altars, Asherah poles, and incense altars in Genesis 8:20, Genesis 13:18, Genesis 26:25, Exodus 20:24, Joshua 8:30, Judges 6:24–26, 2 Kings 23:4–6, 2 Chronicles 34:7, and Isaiah 27:9.]

Day 12:

An Astounding Turnaround

Isaiah 19–20

In that day there will be an altar to the Lord in the heart of Egypt, and a monument to the Lord at its border. Isaiah 19:19

Isaiah often mentions the nation of Egypt in his prophecies. Egypt appears in the book of Isaiah forty-three times. Many, but not all, of these mentions relate to judgment and punishment. In a surprising passage, Isaiah looks forward to the day when Egypt will openly and intentionally embrace God as their Lord.

In the time between Isaiah's prophecy and now, I'm not aware of this spiritual turnaround having happened. And it certainly isn't the situation today. We're still waiting for this prophecy's fulfillment. That means we anticipate a future time when Egypt will turn to God and fear him as their true Lord.

Looking forward, Isaiah sees this coming age when the people of Egypt will erect an altar to God in the heart of their country. In addition, they will place a monument honoring him on their border. This will serve as a witness to all regarding the Lord Almighty. Egypt will pursue a state-sanctioned embrace of biblical God.

Also, they will worship God with sacrifices, grain offerings, and vows. And they won't make their promises in haste. Rather, they'll honor the pledges they make to the Lord God.

How will this come to be?

Isaiah says that Egypt will face a time of oppression. They will call out to God for help. He will send them a savior, a defender, a rescuer. Though this opposition could come from a foreign power, it could also come from above. Isaiah says that God will strike the Egyptians with the plague. Remember, he did this before to get their attention. He sent them ten plagues of increasing severity so that Egypt would give God's enslaved people their freedom.

In the future, God will send one more plague, which will hit Egypt hard. But then he will hear their pleas for help, respond to their agony, and heal them from their affliction. He will save them, defend them, and rescue them.

In this way, he will reveal himself to them. And they will accept him as their Lord.

What might God need to do to get our attention?

[Discover more about Moses and Egypt's plagues in Exodus 6–12.]

Day 13:

Water for the Thirsty

Isaiah 21

A prophecy against Arabia: You caravans of Dedanites, who camp in the thickets of Arabia, bring water for the thirsty; you who live in Tema, bring food for the fugitives.
Isaiah 21:13–14

Isaiah continues his prophecy against various nations. He has more to say about Babylon before he directs his attention briefly to Edom, followed by Arabia.

His words to Arabia emerge as an encouragement to provide humanitarian aid to people running from raised swords and aimed bows. They need help. They're thirsty and hungry. Isaiah tells those nearby to provide water and food for these fugitives. Yes, fugitives. Though they seem like victims, Isaiah calls them fugitives. Interesting. Nevertheless, they need help.

More than any other book in the Bible, Isaiah talks about thirsty people. Other authors also talk about thirsty and hungry people. Here are a few examples:

- After the people leave Egypt and wander in the desert, they become thirsty. Moses miraculously provides them with water to drink.
- As Ruth gleans in the field, Boaz offers water for her to drink whenever she's thirsty.
- The Psalms remind us that God loves us, satisfying us when we're thirsty and filling us when we're hungry—both physically and spiritually.
- In Proverbs, Solomon tells us to feed our enemy if he is hungry and give him water if he is thirsty. This is a hard teaching, but sometimes doing the right thing is difficult.
- Later, Jesus tells us that whenever we feed a hungry person or give water to someone who's

thirsty, it's as if we're doing it for God himself. Interestingly, as Jesus dies on the cross, he says, "I'm thirsty," and someone gives him something to drink.
- And as the Bible wraps up, Revelation promises that God will give the water of life—living water—to the people.

Although regular water temporarily meets a physical need when we're thirsty, living water fills an eternal need to quench our spiritual thirst. In the book of John, Jesus offers living water to the Samaritan woman—and to us.

Before that, Zechariah prophesied about living water flowing out of Jerusalem year-round. This isn't water for physical requirements but living water for spiritual needs. It comes from Jesus and is available to all. The book of Revelation confirms this.

How can we provide water and food to those in physical need? Of eternal consequence, how can we offer living water to those in spiritual need?

[Discover more about thirst and water in Exodus 17:2–7, Ruth 2:9, Psalm 107:8–9, Proverbs 25:21, Matthew 25:34–40, John 19:28–30, Revelation 21:6, and Revelation 22:17. Discover more about living water in Zechariah 14:8, John 4:7–15, John 6:35, John 7:37–38, and Revelation 7:17.]

Day 14:

Eat, Drink, and Be Merry

Isaiah 22

"Let us eat and drink," you say, "for tomorrow we die!" Isaiah 22:13

This time Isaiah's prophecies aren't against Judah's enemies. Instead, he turns his attention to Jerusalem and prophesies about it, the city of David. He talks about the people, his words becoming personal to his audience.

At one point he addresses those who should be in mourning over their dire circumstances. He calls on them to weep, wail, and wear funeral clothes. They don't. Instead, they engage in revelry, feasting, and drinking—doing all three in excess. They exhibit the attitude of "let's eat, drink, and be merry, because tomorrow we could die."

This fatalistic, live-for-today approach to life makes sense for someone who concludes they have no future, not on earth now or in heaven later. If we don't believe in God or hold on to hope in him for the afterlife, why not adopt a live-for-the-moment lifestyle? For those who lack purpose, this makes sense.

It's also unwise. For one, it displeases God. For another, it's shortsighted. And last, it reveals hopelessness when we have every reason to anticipate a better tomorrow in God and through God.

This live-for-today attitude, however, isn't unique to the people of Judah with their enemies pressing in against them. Centuries earlier, we read of Solomon pondering deeply the meaning and purpose of life. For twelve chapters in the book of Ecclesiastes, Solomon records his pursuits of pleasure, waffles in his deliberations, and dips into hopelessness.

At one point he theorizes that the best thing people can do is eat, drink, and find satisfaction in their work, affirming it as a gift from God. Then he says it four more times, the last two with a twist of doing so with gladness and joy. This is his recipe for enjoying life, noting that joy will come to those who work their whole lives, all the days that God has given them.

Long after Solomon and Isaiah, Paul in his first letter to the church in Corinth, cites Isaiah's words about "eat, drink, and die" for those who have no hope of a heavenly future. Then he shakes them back to right thinking. "Don't be fooled." He begs them to come back to their senses and stop sinning. He goes as far as to say that they're ignorant about God and his ways. Paul leaves no doubt that he has a purpose beyond eating and drinking. And he wants us to share in that purpose too.

Solomon concurs. After sharing the pursuits he tried and meandering through his stream of consciousness, he ends his book with a concise conclusion we don't want to miss. He says our duty is to fear God and obey him. Then trust him with the rest.

Do we live for today or for eternity?

[Discover more about eating and drinking for today in Ecclesiastes 2:24, Ecclesiastes 3:13, Ecclesiastes 8:15, and 1 Corinthians 15:32–34. Read about Solomon's conclusion about the purpose of life in Ecclesiastes 12:13–14.]

Dig Deeper:

Isaiah in the New Testament

This was to fulfill the word of Isaiah the prophet: "Lord, who has believed our message and to whom has the arm of the Lord been revealed?" John 12:38

Of all the prophets, the New Testament refers to Isaiah's writing more than any other, with seventy-nine mentions. This may be the reason so many people revere Isaiah's words. The only Old Testament book cited more often in the New Testament than Isaiah is Psalms, at eighty-one times.

Here are the passages in Isaiah that New Testament writers quote, paraphrase, or reference.

> Isaiah 1:9 is in Romans 9:29.
> Isaiah 6:3 is in Revelation 4:8.
> Isaiah 6:9 is in Luke 8:10.
> Isaiah 6:9–10 is in Mark 4:12, Matthew 13:13–15, and Acts 28:26–27.

Isaiah 6:10 is in John 12:40.

Isaiah 7:14 is in Matthew 1:23.

Isaiah 8:12 is in 1 Peter 3:14.

Isaiah 8:14 is in Romans 9:33 and 1 Peter 2:8.

Isaiah 8:17 is in Hebrews 2:13.

Isaiah 8:18 is in Hebrews 2:13.

Isaiah 9:1–2 is in Matthew 4:15–16.

Isaiah 10:22–23 is in Romans 9:27–28.

Isaiah 11:10 is in Romans 15:12.

Isaiah 13:10 is in Matthew 24:29 and Mark 13:24–25.

Isaiah 21:9 is in Revelation 14:8 and Revelation 18:2.

Isaiah 22:13 is in 1 Corinthians 15:32.

Isaiah 25:8 is in 1 Corinthians 15:54, Revelation 7:17, and Revelation 21:4.

Isaiah 27:9 is in Romans 11:27.

Isaiah 28:11–12 is in 1 Corinthians 14:21.

Isaiah 28:16 is in Romans 9:33, 1 Peter 2:6, and Romans 10:11.

Isaiah 29:10 is in Romans 11:8.

Isaiah 29:13 is in Matthew 15:8–9 and Mark 7:6–7.

Isaiah 29:14 is in 1 Corinthians 1:19.

Isaiah 29:16 is in Romans 9:20.

Isaiah 34:4 is in Matthew 24:2, Mark 13:25, and Revelation 6:13.

Isaiah 40:3 is in Matthew 3:3, Mark 1:3, and John 1:23.

Isaiah 40:3–5 is in Luke 3:4–6.

Isaiah 40:6–8 is in 1 Peter 1:24–25.

Isaiah 40:13 is in Romans 11:34 and 1 Corinthians 2:16.

Isaiah 42:1–4 is in Matthew 12:17–21.

Isaiah 45:9 is in Romans 9:20.

Isaiah 45:23 is in Romans 14:11.

Isaiah 47:7–8 is in Revelation 18:7.

Isaiah 49:6 is in Luke 2:32 and Acts 13:47.

Isaiah 49:8 is in 2 Corinthians 6:2.

Isaiah 49:10 is in Revelation 7:16–17.

Isaiah 52:5 is in Romans 2:24.

Isaiah 52:7 is in Romans 10:15.

Isaiah 52:11 is in 2 Corinthians 6:17.

Isaiah 52:15 is in Romans 15:21.

Isaiah 53:1 is in John 12:38 and Romans 10:16.

Isaiah 53:4 is in Matthew 8:17.

Isaiah 53:4–6 is in 1 Peter 2:24–25.

Isaiah 53:7–8 is in Acts 8:32–33.

Isaiah 53:9 is in 1 Peter 2:22.
Isaiah 53:12 is in Luke 22:37.
Isaiah 54:1 is in Galatians 4:27.
Isaiah 54:13 is in John 6:45.
Isaiah 55:3 is in Acts 13:34.
Isaiah 56:7 is in Matthew 21:13, Mark 11:17, and Luke 19:46.
Isaiah 58:6 is in Luke 4:18–19.
Isaiah 59:7–8 is in Romans 3:15–17.
Isaiah 59:20–21 is in Romans 11:26–27.
Isaiah 61:1–2 is in Luke 4:18–19.
Isaiah 64:4 is in 1 Corinthians 2:9.
Isaiah 65:1 is in Romans 10:20.
Isaiah 65:2 is in Romans 10:21.
Isaiah 65:17 is in Revelation 21:1.
Isaiah 66:1–2 is in Acts 7:49–50.
Isaiah 66:24 is in Mark 9:48.

How can the words of Isaiah strengthen our faith today and inform our actions?

[Discover more about Isaiah in 2 Kings 19:2–7, 2 Kings 20:16–17, 2 Chronicles 26:22, 2 Chronicles 32:20–21, and 2 Chronicles 32:32.]

Day 15:

Seventy Years

Isaiah 23

At that time Tyre will be forgotten for seventy years, the span of a king's life. . . . At the end of seventy years, the Lord will deal with Tyre. She will return to her lucrative prostitution and will ply her trade with all the kingdoms on the face of the earth. Isaiah 23:15 and 17

Moses says in a psalm—yes, Moses wrote a psalm—that we normally live seventy years or even up to eighty. (Interestingly, he lived to 120.) Pegging a typical lifespan at seventy years, that number comes up in today's reading.

Isaiah prophesies against the city of Tyre. With a Mediterranean port, Tyre is a hub of commerce, activity . . . and reveling. Isaiah predicts the destruction of Tyre. There will be no more trade. The reveling will end.

Yet Tyre's destruction won't last forever. It's merely a timeout, albeit a seventy-year one. This is the span of the king's life, the length of most everyone's life. That means most of the people who knew of Tyre before its destruction will die before its restoration. And those present when its timeout ends will have no idea of the prosperity it once enjoyed.

Isaiah, however, doesn't celebrate their return as a center of commerce. Instead, he declares that Tyre will return to her profitable prostitution. This may be an implied warning to us to make sure that while conducting business we don't sell out ourselves—or our souls.

Tyre isn't the only place to get a seventy-year timeout. The nation of Judah will get one too. Jeremiah, who follows Isaiah by about fifty years, will prophesy a seventy-year timeout for Judah. This isn't a reprieve. Its time spent in the penalty box.

God has been trying to get the attention of his people for centuries, but they continually ignore him.

Although they experience momentary times when they worship and obey him, mostly they turn their backs on him and test his patience.

God has finally had enough. He will take a more drastic approach. Babylon will invade Judah, destroy its infrastructure, and relocate most of the people to regions throughout Babylon. Then, after seventy years pass and most of the people have died, their descendants will witness Babylon's fall. After that God will bring his people home.

But before this return occurs, our story will shift to Daniel. He is one of the people in Judah who ends up being deported to Babylon. He may have been a teen at the time or even a young lad. Though removed from his family and taken from his homeland, Daniel conducts himself well in Babylon. He rises to a position of influence, advising multiple leaders over a span of several decades.

Daniel understands Jeremiah's prophecy about the seventy years. When the time is about up, Daniel seeks God through prayer and fasting. Soon God's people return to Judah.

Regardless of whether God gives us seventy years to live or not, what will we do to make our time here on earth count for him?

[Discover more about seventy years in Psalm 90:10, Jeremiah 25:8–12, Jeremiah 29:10, and Daniel 9:2–3.]

Day 16:

The End Times

Isaiah 24

In that day the Lord will punish the powers in the heavens above and the kings on the earth below. Isaiah 24:21

In most biblical prophecies, the foretelling bounces from one era to another. Some prophecies look to the near future, others consider the intermediate future, and a few concern the far-off future. This is true for Isaiah's prophecies.

For example, consider the time frame in Day 8: "The Arrogant Will Fall" and Day 15: "Seventy Years." These prophecies address Isaiah's near future. Sometimes a prophet's near-future predictions happen in his lifetime, though most happen shortly thereafter.

Both Day 4: "A Sign" and Day 5: "A Child Is Born" look at the intermediate future, at least from Isaiah's perspective. They anticipate Jesus's coming to his people as a baby. His arrival fulfills Isaiah's prophecies several hundred years after the prophet's death.

From our perspective today, both these near-term and intermediate predictions have already occurred. That leaves prophecies for the far-off future. For this, we have Day 12: "An Astounding Turnaround" and Day 17: "My Holy Mountain." We're still waiting to see these fulfilled two and a half millennia after Isaiah foresaw it. Prophecy that fits squarely in this far-off foretelling category is end-time predictions.

Today's passage is one of those far-off prophecies, even though Isaiah may have no idea where it fits in the future timeline. This may explain why it's stuck in the middle of the book of Isaiah and not at the end, where it logically belongs—or at least where we think it ought to be.

In this prophecy, Isaiah looks at the end of life as we know it. Our planet will lie in waste, devastated and plundered. People will scatter, full of guilt for the lives they lived—or didn't live. Most will die by fire (an allusion to hell?), with only a few remaining who will survive. This understanding devastates Isaiah. He has the second of his woe-is-me moments.

But there's more. God will exact punishment on much of his creation. This includes those who orchestrate havoc in the spiritual realm and those who rule poorly in the physical realm. Together God will toss them into a dungeon and lock the doors tight. Though the earthly devastation will dismay the moon and embarrass the sun, God will reign supreme, ruling with great glory.

But lest we mourn these events, this isn't the end but a new beginning. We don't know when the end will occur—Jesus says only the Father knows—but what we do know is that it will be a good beginning—at least for us.

How should we treat prophecies of the end times?

[Discover more about the end times in Matthew 24:36, Mark 13:32, Revelation 19:20, and Revelation 20:2.]

Dig Deeper:

The Ethiopian Treasurer Reads Isaiah

On his way home [he] was sitting in his chariot reading the Book of Isaiah the prophet. The Spirit told Philip, "Go to that chariot and stay near it." Acts 8:28–29

A man from Ethiopia makes a pilgrimage to Jerusalem. He's a high-ranking official in the Ethiopian government, the treasurer to the Kandake, the Queen of the Ethiopian people. The Bible also tells us that he's a eunuch. This doesn't seem like a relevant piece of information, yet history has pinned this label on the Ethiopian treasurer.

Taking a leave of absence from work, the Ethiopian treasurer travels to Jerusalem to worship God. Once he wraps up, he heads home. It's a long journey, but he has his chariot to make the trip easier and faster. Along the way, he pulls out a scroll—he must have been super rich to own a scroll—and reads from Isaiah's prophecy. Though intrigued, he can't make sense of it.

That's when Philip strolls up and asks if the Ethiopian man has any questions. Boy, does he.

Though we don't know what passage he's reading, we do know it looks forward to Jesus, but the Ethiopian can't wrap his mind around it. "Is Isaiah talking about himself or someone else?"

Building on that passage, Philip tells the man about Jesus. Then things start to click. They travel along the road as Philip teaches his new friend. When they come to some water, the Ethiopian treasurer asks Philip to baptize him. Philip does, but when the Ethiopian rises out of the water, Philip is gone.

Unshaken, the Ethiopian treasurer continues his journey home, full of joy for what God has done for him through Jesus.

How ready are we to explain Isaiah's prophecy to someone else? If we're not, will we rely on the Holy Spirit to guide our words?

[Discover more about the Ethiopian official in Acts 8:26–39.]

Day 17:

My Holy Mountain

Isaiah 25

On this mountain the Lord Almighty will prepare a feast of rich food for all peoples.
Isaiah 25:6

Isaiah has just predicted the end of the world. What does he do? Mourn over the loss he just foretold? Play a funeral dirge? Give up, fall into a deep depression, and mope? Nope.

He sings. Yep. Isaiah writes another psalm, his second one. He celebrates who God is and what he will do. Isaiah praises God as Lord and affirms what he did, actions he planned long ago (I suspect before the beginning of time). All of this praise and affirmation emerge as powerful worship to the Sovereign Lord, the God Almighty.

In this psalm, Isaiah also talks about a special place: God's mountain. In fact, throughout the book of Isaiah, the prophet talks a lot about mountains. He mentions mountains more often than any other writer in the Bible. Though some of the occurrences of mountains in Isaiah's writing refer to a regular mountain, many of the mentions indicate God's mountain in Jerusalem (Zion) as in *the* mountain, *my* mountain, *this* mountain, and *my holy* mountain. It's on *this holy mountain* that Jesus will rule all the nations.

Here are some of the things we can anticipate on this mountain:

- God, the Lord Almighty, will provide a feast there for all people. This grand banquet will provide the tastiest food and choicest wine. Though this references grand nourishment for our physical bodies, it implies sustenance for our spiritual being too.
- God—through Jesus—will overcome death forever. He'll swallow it up, gone for good. He'll destroy death, which once affected all people but not anymore.

- God—our Sovereign Lord—will remove our sorrows. He'll comfort us and dry our tears.
- And with our tears gone, God will remove the shame of his people—not all people but *his* people, those who follow and believe in him.

How do we know this? We know it because God spoke it through Isaiah. That means we can count on it.

But there's more. On this mountain we'll affirm him as Lord. We placed our trust in him, and he saved us. And to make sure we grasp this thought, Isaiah repeats this truth of trust followed by salvation. In this, and because of this, we will praise God.

Thank you, Lord, for saving us. We will rejoice and be glad.

Do we fully trust God for our eternal salvation?

[Discover more about God's holy mountain in Psalm 2:6, Isaiah 11:9, Isaiah 56:7, Isaiah 57:13, Isaiah 65:11, Isaiah 65:25, Isaiah 66:20, and Ezekiel 20:40.]

Day 18:

The Desire of Our Hearts

Isaiah 26

Your name and renown are the desire of our hearts. Isaiah 26:8

Isaiah has just foretold the end of an era, of life as he knows it. Then he surprises us by ignoring the somber nature of his prophecy. Instead, he writes a song of praise to God, another psalm, his third overall. But this one isn't for him or the people he knows. It's for future generations.

When God ushers in his new beginning on his holy mountain, we'll sing our praises to him. To make sure we're ready, Isaiah prepares this psalm in advance. Imagine composing a piece that no one will perform for several thousand years. That's some confident planning. That's faith that God will do what he says he will do. And as he writes, Isaiah envisions himself there for its unveiling, singing along with the rest of us.

One line of Isaiah's song jumps out at me. It seems out of place. In his song, Isaiah writes that God is the desire of our hearts. We yearn for him during the night, and we long for him when we awaken. This reminds me of the Song of Songs. In Solomon's poem—which we can read like a modern-day screenplay—the king writes about the passionate, clandestine, desire between two lovers. The text oozes with a near-primal craving the pair has for each other, to hold each other in a tight embrace and never let go.

Embedded in this physical love story between man and woman resides a spiritual love story between us and God. It can emerge—it should emerge—just as primal, just as urgent, and just as essential. We are Jesus's beloved, his betrothed. We are the bride of Christ.

Some people, especially men, squirm at the implication of being married to Jesus. This might be because we haven't seen enough positive examples of marriage in our world, but it's more likely that we focus on the physical act of marriage and not the spiritual part.

This imagery of being Jesus's bride does not imply physical intimacy. Instead, it points to the even more significant spiritual closeness he desires to have with us. May we yearn for a deep, meaningful spiritual intimacy with Jesus even more so than we pursue human physical affection.

How deep, urgent, and essential is our spiritual intimacy with Jesus?

[Discover more about God's love for us and our being the bride of Christ in Matthew 9:15, Matthew 25:1–13, John 3:29, 2 Corinthians 11:2, Revelation 19:7–9, Revelation 21:2, Revelation 21:9–10, and Revelation 22:17, and well as the entire book of Song of Songs.]

Day 19:

Going Home

Isaiah 27

And in that day a great trumpet will sound. Those who were perishing in Assyria and those who were exiled in Egypt will come and worship the Lord on the holy mountain in Jerusalem. Isaiah 27:13

After writing his psalms of praise to God, Isaiah continues the positivity by looking forward to the day when his people will receive deliverance from their enemies. Though the people view this as a physical rescue, many people today understand it as a spiritual one. In both cases we look forward to the time when we go home, either in body or in spirit.

Three times in Isaiah 27, he says, "in that day," referring to God's future rescue of his people. Each time, he uses this phrase to introduce a section of this prophecy, with the second part of three being the longest and most poetic. But it's in the last section that we find a most encouraging proclamation.

On this long-anticipated day of deliverance, the trumpet call will reverberate throughout the land. God's people living in exile will return home. Some have been languishing in Assyria, which conquered Israel in the middle of Isaiah's ministry and deported many Israelites to Assyria.

Others sit exiled in Egypt. Though Jeremiah ends up there, it won't be for another 150 years. His own people will drag him there as they flee Judea to avoid capture by the Babylonians. It could be that Isaiah is looking forward in time, prophetically referring to Jeremiah and his crew. Or it could be that others have already fled to Egypt to escape the Assyrians. Regardless, this prophecy looks forward to when it's time for them to return home.

When they come home, they'll worship God on his holy mountain in Jerusalem. (See Day 17: "My Holy Mountain.") Imagine living far from home. Then after years of longing to return to the country of your birth and your youth, you finally get a chance to go. And in this great homecoming, you worship God as the giver of this gift: your repatriation, both physically and spiritually.

In our spiritual homecoming, however, we'll return to our Creator, spending eternity with him in heaven. What a glorious reunion this will be. We anticipate this in great expectation, and increasingly so for people as they grow older and their time to go home draws near.

A more tangible understanding of this homecoming appears in one of Jesus's parables. We often call this The Parable of the Prodigal Son or The Lost Son. After turning his back on his father and squandering his share of the inheritance on carnal pleasures, this young man realizes he needs to return home and seek his father's forgiveness. He slinks back in shame over what he has done with his life and how he disrespected his dad. He plans to grovel and ask for the smallest of mercies.

Meanwhile, his father has been scanning the horizon, watching for his son's return for a long time. As soon as he spots him, Dad runs out to meet his boy, embracing him and kissing him. The father dismisses his boy's request for forgiveness as irrelevant. Instead,

Dad reinstates his son as a member of the family, an heir to all he has. He throws a massive party in celebration of his boy's return.

So it will be when we see Jesus in heaven, after the end of our time here on earth.

What do we expect our eternal homecoming to look like? Are we excited or nervous?

[Discover more about going home in Ecclesiastes 12:5, Ezekiel 36:8, and Luke 15:11–32.]

Dig Deeper:

The Leviathan

In that day, the Lord will punish with his sword—his fierce, great and powerful sword—Leviathan the gliding serpent, Leviathan the coiling serpent; he will slay the monster of the sea. Isaiah 27:1

Isaiah refers to an animal called Leviathan. We don't know what kind of creature it is, but it shows up six times in the Bible: three times in Job, twice in Psalms, and once here in Isaiah.

From these six accounts, we can piece together some ideas about Leviathan. It's a sea creature of terrifying presence. One passage talks of its limbs, strength, and grace. Isaiah calls it a serpent.

There are three thoughts about Leviathan. One is that it is a mythological creature that never existed. It represents an evil force, possibly Satan.

The second understanding is that Leviathan is an ancestor of today's crocodile.

A third view is that Leviathan was a real animal that is now extinct. But don't think that it died during the great flood. First, as a sea animal, water wouldn't kill it. Second, all six of the Bible's Leviathan mentions occur in books written after Noah and the flood.

We'll never know for sure. What Leviathan was and represents remains for us to ponder. It's one more mystery of God that we can contemplate. Though we don't know now, this—and all of God's other mysteries—will one day become clear. It certainly won't be the first thing I ask God about when I get to heaven, but I do intend to ask.

What is the first question you'll ask God when you get to heaven?

[Discover more about Leviathan in Job 3:8, Job 41:1, Psalm 74:13–14, and Psalm 104:26.]

Day 20:

A Precious Cornerstone

Isaiah 28

"See, I lay a stone in Zion, a tested stone, a precious cornerstone for a sure foundation; the one who relies on it will never be stricken with panic." Isaiah 28:16

In one short, quick verse, Isaiah smartly and prophetically summarizes Jesus and what he will accomplish during his time on earth. But these aren't Isaiah's words. They are God's. Isaiah merely records the words that the Lord speaks to him.

God says that he will erect a stone as the foundation of Zion (Jerusalem), his church. The stone stands as tested, precious, and sure. God calls it a cornerstone. Everyone who relies on this cornerstone will never have a reason to panic.

In today's architecture, we view a cornerstone as a symbolic piece of a building, often used to ceremonially mark the beginning of construction. It usually has the year engraved on it in a visual tribute to the building. The expectation is that the building will endure as a monument. But this cornerstone is visual, not structural. This is not the type of cornerstone Isaiah refers to.

A more historical understanding of a cornerstone is an essential foundational element that sits at the intersection of two key walls of the building. It's integral. Upon the cornerstone sit two vital interconnected walls. Builders select this cornerstone with care. If it's the wrong size or quality, everything built upon it is at risk. A good cornerstone is a foundation for a building that lasts. A poor cornerstone could easily bring about a building's ruin.

New Testament writers often cite Isaiah 28:16 about God's cornerstone. In their biographies of Jesus, Matthew, Mark, and Luke all write of Jesus quoting this verse. Later in Acts, Peter speaks before the Sanhedrin. Though he has an opportunity to defend his and John's arrest for telling others about Jesus, the Holy Spirit directs him to give a mini sermon.

He quotes this verse from Isaiah and adds that only through the cornerstone of Jesus's name can anyone receive salvation. Peter again uses this verse in his first letter, whereas Paul refers to it in his dispatch to the Ephesians. That makes six New Testament references to this one Old Testament verse.

Isaiah hit a home run when he wrote this foundational verse. Actually, credit for the home run goes to God, for he spoke this message for Isaiah to write down.

Jesus is the spiritual cornerstone of our faith. He is the cornerstone sent to us from Father God. In him we place our trust. On him we can rely—both now and eternally.

What do we do to treat Jesus as our cornerstone?

[Discover more about cornerstones in Job 38:6, Psalm 118:22-23, Zechariah 10:4, Matthew 21:42, Mark 12:10, Luke 20:17, Acts 4:8-12, Ephesians 2:19-21, and 1 Peter 2:6-7.]

Day 21:

Going through the Motions

Isaiah 29

The Lord says: "These people come near to me with their mouth and honor me with their lips, but their hearts are far from me. Their worship of me is based on merely human rules they have been taught." Isaiah 29:13

As Isaiah continues writing his prophecy, he records the words of God. God criticizes the people for their wrong approach to worshiping him. The people go through the motions of paying him homage. Their mouths say the right words, but they are idle utterances. They don't mean what they say. Their hearts aren't in it. This disrespects God and disappoints him.

Beyond that, their worship comes from man-made rules, which their religious leaders have taught them and passed down from one generation to the next. They strayed from God's instructions on right worship and replaced his ways with their own traditions that make them feel good. But this falls short of God's desires for their worship, and it misses out on having a relationship with him.

This sounds a lot like the Pharisees in Jesus's day. He often criticizes their hypocrisy. Over the centuries they developed thousands of principles to help them apply the Law of Moses with precision. But in doing so, they missed the point. They think following their rules will guide them into a right relationship with God. Instead, it drives a wedge between them, distancing them from the God who wants them close.

Jesus talks about hypocrites on several occasions, with the word popping up often in the book of Matthew, especially in chapter 23. Jesus even quotes today's passage from the book of Isaiah, applying it to the Pharisees and religious leaders who have it all wrong and lead others astray in the process.

One of the most visual of Jesus's criticisms of the Pharisees refers to those who point out a speck in someone else's eye—a small problem or perceived issue. Yet the Pharisees can't help these people because they have a board lodged in their own eyes—a big problem that obscures their ability to see and to help.

Jesus also condemns the Pharisees for calling attention to themselves when they give money to the poor. In addition, they recite grandiose prayers to make themselves look good in front of others. And when they fast, they don't do so privately. Rather, they make a good show of it to garner pity for their sacrifice. This is the only reward they will receive because God is not impressed with their showy, outwardly focused pretenses of worship.

Jesus continues to expose their hypocrisy. They don't know how to worship God, and they replaced the relationship he desires with the rules they made up. It's easy for us to see their faults and shortcomings.

What's hard for us to see is the way we do the same things today. I fear we're as much of a hypocrite as the Pharisees in Jesus's time and the people in Isaiah's day. We must do better. We've received our warning. Now we must change how we worship God.

Are we going through the motions when we worship God?

[Discover more about hypocrites in Psalm 26:4, Matthew 6:1–6, Matthew 6:16–18, Matthew 7:4–5, Matthew 15:7–20, Matthew 23:1–30, Mark 7:6–7, and Luke 13:10–17.]

Dig Deeper:

The Potter and the Clay

You turn things upside down, as if the potter were thought to be like the clay! Shall what is formed say to the one who formed it, "You did not make me"? Can the pot say to the potter, "You know nothing"? Isaiah 29:16

Isaiah often uses the imagery of a potter and clay as a metaphor to understand our relationship with God. He's not the only prophet to do so. Jeremiah uses it also.

The potter forms a lump of clay into whatever he or she wishes. It can be a beautiful bowl for special use or something common. And if the potter doesn't like how it's turning out, he can start over and make something different. The potter is the creator, and the clay is his creation. The clay fully depends on the wishes of the potter. From the perspective of the clay, the potter is sovereign, someone who is supreme in authority and operates with complete independence.

God is the potter, and we are his clay. He is sovereign over how to make us, treat us, and use us.

How do we feel about the metaphor that God is our potter and we are his clay?

[Discover more about the potter and the clay in Isaiah 45:9, Isaiah 64:8, Jeremiah 18:2–6, Lamentations 4:2, and Romans 9:21.]

Day 22:

Lie to Us

Isaiah 30–31

*They say to the seers, "See no more visions!"
and to the prophets, "Give us no more visions
of what is right! Tell us pleasant things,
prophesy illusions.* Isaiah 30:10

Can we handle the truth?

How do we react when we come across a Bible passage we don't like? Yes, there are verses we love because they offer us comfort and hope. And there are sections that confuse us, so we usually skim over them. But what about the verses we don't like? Most people ignore them or try to explain them away with some convoluted "logic" that no one really accepts. In doing so, we effectively cut those words out of our Bible. Instead of having a Holy Bible, we have a Bible with holes.

The same situation can occur at church during the message. How do we respond when a minister tells us something we don't want to hear? Most people dismiss words that offend, words that correct, and words that convict. They instead choose to hold on to nice-sounding one-liners that make them feel good and affirm their actions and beliefs. But they close their ears to messages that make them feel bad or confront their wrong thinking or actions.

Some church boards and influential church members have even told preachers to not mention certain topics. These themes might address sins that offend some people. Or they could be subjects that are politically incorrect. And in this world of political correctness, many choose to avoid saying anything that people might perceive as inappropriate or take offense at, especially God's truth that may sound critical or intolerant.

This bad idea isn't new.

The people in Isaiah's day encountered this same situation. God criticizes these people as rebellious, deceitful, and unwilling to listen to his words. These people tell their prophets to knock it off. "Stop telling us your visions," they say. "And we're especially offended when you tell us what is right."

They have a better idea. They want to hear only nice things. They'd rather hear an illusion than the truth. They want their prophets to lie to them. "We don't like the direction you're going with your message," they say. "Stop confronting us with our shortcomings and say nice things instead."

But a true prophet, and a true minister, must speak God's truth regardless if it's unpopular or the audience doesn't want to hear it.

How do we react when we encounter a biblical truth that makes us squirm?

[Discover more about taking offense to God's Word in Micah 2:6, Micah 2:11, Micah 3:5, Matthew 13:57, Mark 6:2–5, and John 6:60–66.]

Day 23:

Who Is Our Lord?

Isaiah 32–33

For the Lord is our judge, the Lord is our lawgiver, the Lord is our king; it is he who will save us. Isaiah 33:22

When I come across the word *Lord* in the Bible—which occurs over six thousand times and appears in almost every book—I'm never quite sure how to interpret it. The dictionary says that I can understand *Lord* to mean God or Jesus. Hence my confusion. Which one is it? Is it both? Or could it be that it doesn't matter because Jesus is part of the Godhead, along with the Father and Holy Spirit?

Today's passage will not directly answer my dilemma, but it does give a better understanding of who the Lord is and what he does.

First, the Lord judges us. He's our Judge. A judge—at least an ethical one, which is how I perceive God—makes determinations between right and wrong. As our Judge, our Lord God looks at what we have done and makes a legal determination of our case. Should we receive a reprieve or a sentence? Since everyone sins, we all fall short of perfection and deserve punishment. But as our Judge, the Lord God can offer us mercy: not getting the penalty we deserve.

Second, the Lord gives us laws. He's our Lawgiver. These laws fall into two categories: things we're supposed to do and things we're not supposed to do. In the Old Testament, the Law of Moses contains 613 commands—things to do or not do. Unfortunately, we can never fully obey all these directives. We all fall short of following the law perfectly, which separates us from God. Therefore, we need a different solution to be reconciled to him.

Third, the Lord rules over us. He's our King. A king is a supreme ruler over a group of people. He is preeminent. He is sovereign. That means a king can do whatever he wants. What he says, goes. Some kings rule with a firm hand and others with a gentle embrace. For those people who uphold democracy as the ideal form of government, the idea of a king is an old-fashioned concept. It seems out of date and out of touch. Yet the Lord God is our King.

Last, and most important, our Lord will rescue us. He's our Savior. As our Judge, the Lord will find us lacking. As our Lawgiver, we can't meet his expectations. And as our King, our Lord can punish us or offer us mercy. That's why we need a Savior, and our Lord will save us.

It doesn't matter if we perceive the Lord as God or as Jesus, the bottom line is that our Lord saves.

Do we trust our Lord to save us?

[Discover more about the Lord in Psalm 23:1, Luke 1:30–33, Acts 4:33, 2 Corinthians 6:18, James 5:11, Revelation 1:8, and Revelation 4:8.]

Dig Deeper:

Other Nations

Come near, you nations, and listen; pay attention, you peoples! Let the earth hear, and all that is in it, the world, and all that comes out of it! Isaiah 34:1

Isaiah prophesies from Judah. Many of his words are for the people of Judah (directly mentioned twenty-eight times) and especially Israel (mentioned ninety-four times). Together, these two nations comprise God's chosen people.

However, Isaiah also has words of criticism and prophecy for other nations and cities. Note that often prophecies against a city or capital apply to the entire nation.

Here are the major references to these countries and the total number of times they're mentioned in the book of Isaiah:

- Arabia (Isaiah 21:13–17, mentioned once)
- Assyria, which conquered Israel during Isaiah's lifetime (Isaiah 7:18–25, Isaiah 10:5–19, and Isaiah 31:8–9, mentioned a total of forty-one times in Isaiah)
- Babylon, which later conquered Judah (Isaiah 13:1–22, Isaiah 21:1–10, Isaiah 39:1–8, Isaiah 46:1–13, and Isaiah 47:1–15, eighteen times)
- Cush (Isaiah 18:1–7 and Isaiah 20:1–6, nine times)
- Aram, represented by the city of Damascus (Isaiah 7:1–9 and Isaiah 17:1–14, six times for Aram and five times for Damascus)
- Edom (Isaiah 21:11–12, seven times)
- Egypt (Isaiah 19:1–25 and Isaiah 31:1–3, forty-three times)
- Moab (Isaiah 15:1–16:14, seventeen times)
- The Philistines (Isaiah 14:28–32, five times)
- Tyre, which was a major town in Phoenicia (Isaiah 23:1–18, six times for Tyre and once for Phoenicia)
- The whole earth, all nations, others (Isaiah 24:1–23, Isaiah 34:1–17, and Isaiah 56:1–8, one time each)

What is our perspective of God's view of other nations and people?

[Discover more about God's plan for all people in Matthew 28:19, Mark 11:17, Mark 13:10, Luke 2:30–32, Galatians 3:8, and Revelation 15:4.]

Day 24:

A Future Healing

Isaiah 34–35

Then will the eyes of the blind be opened and the ears of the deaf unstopped. Then will the lame leap like a deer, and the mute tongue shout for joy. Isaiah 35:5–6

Amid the doom and the gloom in the book of Isaiah, we also see a reason for hope and the source for joy. Isaiah looks forward to a future time of healing and restoration. People who can't see will see. People who can't hear will hear. People who can't walk will leap. And people who can't talk will shout with joy. How exciting is this? Hallelujah!

Though the Old Testament has some accounts of people receiving supernatural healing from their ailments, Jesus exemplifies this future vision of people with impairments being healed so that they can see, hear, walk, and talk. (And later his disciples continued in this mission of physical restoration.)

Jesus often helps people with physical needs. Then they're open for him to help them spiritually too. Restoring people's sight, hearing, mobility, and speech certainly gets their attention, as well as the crowds who witness these healings.

Jesus does more than restore health. He casts out evil spirits. Regardless of how we understand this, the point is that Jesus makes people's lives better. He also raises the dead. Even himself.

But the abilities Isaiah mentions—sight, hearing, mobility, and speech—are all physical concerns. Let's take a moment to consider seeing and hearing from a spiritual perspective. Jesus often concludes his parables by saying, "Whoever has ears, let them hear."

Another time, Jesus said that the people have hard hearts. They can't comprehend spiritual concepts. They can hardly hear, and they shut their eyes tight. They can't grasp what Jesus is saying or see what he is doing. If they could, their hearts would understand, and Jesus would heal them.

Therefore, Jesus proclaims blessings on people who can see and hear spiritual truth. And to those who can't, he says calluses cover their hearts, making them hard. He adds that their hearts and ears are uncircumcised (that is, unable to feel and hear God). Calling them uncircumcised, even figuratively, is a major insult to the Jews in his audience. As a result, they resist the work of God's Holy Spirit. They're in a spiritual stupor.

May we all have ears to hear and eyes to see.

Are we able to see God at work? Are we able to hear his message to us?

[Discover more about what the New Testament says about seeing and hearing in Matthew 13:15–16, Mark 4:9, Mark 8:18, Luke 10:23–24, Acts 7:51, Acts 28:27, Romans 11:7–8, and Revelation 13:9.]

Day 25:

Where's Your Confidence?

Isaiah 36–37

"Tell Hezekiah: 'This is what the great king, the king of Assyria, says: On what are you basing this confidence of yours?'" Isaiah 36:4

Starting with Isaiah 36, this otherwise prophetic book switches to a narrative for four chapters, talking about King Hezekiah. (See Dig Deeper: "A Historical Account.")

King Hezekiah, a direct descendant of King David, rules the nation of Judah from the city of Jerusalem. Things aren't going well for him or the nation. The king of Assyria has set out to conquer Judah and has Jerusalem under siege. Vastly outnumbered, Judah possesses limited resources and holds no reasonable hope for victory. From a human perspective, they're in a hopeless situation with no expectation of winning.

Outside the city wall, the Assyrian field commander calls out to King Hezekiah—and everyone in the city who can hear. He mocks the king for his faith in God. "What's the basis for your confidence?" he shouts. The field commander scornfully asks if Hezekiah is depending on God to save him, the city, and his nation. "Given your situation, your words are an empty boast." Then he gives some sources of assurance that seem wise from a human perspective, such as the strategy of military advisors or a powerful ally—namely Egypt.

King Hezekiah is relying on God, but he commands his people to not react to their enemy's taunts.

Then the field commander appeals to the people. "Don't listen to your king. Your God can't save you." The commander promises if they surrender, he will relocate them to a new land with plenty to eat and drink.

King Hezekiah freaks out. He goes into the temple and seeks God, begging him to save them from the overwhelming forces of their enemy. He prays for deliverance, and God comes through. He sends an angel who wipes out the Assyrian army. And later the king of Assyria is assassinated.

God miraculously rescues his people from their enemy. And they didn't need to do a single thing except seek him.

Though we might not be in a city under siege and facing death, God can come through for us during our dark times, whatever they may be, just as he did for Hezekiah and the people in Jerusalem. We can trust God and place our confidence in him for deliverance. We can seek him, and he will save us.

In whom or what do we place our confidence?

[Discover more about godly confidence in Psalm 71:5, Jeremiah 17:7, Ezekiel 29:16, Romans 15:13, Ephesians 3:12, Philippians 3:2–11, and 1 Peter 2:6.]

Dig Deeper:

A Historical Account

Since I myself have carefully investigated everything from the beginning, I too decided to write an orderly account for you, most excellent Theophilus. Luke 1:3

We classify the book of Isaiah as a prophetic book, which tells what will be. This is unlike the historical books of the Bible that relay the details of what was. However, contrary to the genre, the book of Isaiah includes four chapters that are historic rather than prophetic. Interestingly, the main content of these four historic chapters occurs in two other places in the Bible as well. (Additional genre-defying content in Isaiah are three psalms. See Day 8: "Isaiah's Psalm of Praise", Day 17: "My Holy Mountain", and Day 18: "The Desire of Our Hearts".)

Four of the historical books of the Bible are 1 Samuel, 2 Samuel, 1 Kings, and 2 Kings. They tell us about all the rulers of Israel and of Judah. They start with the life of Israel's first king, Saul, and go all the way through to Judah's last king, Jehoiachin. Parallel to this quartet of books are two other historical books: 1 Chronicles and 2 Chronicles. These books focus on the kings of Judah.

These two sets of historical books cover overlapping information, including the reign of King Hezekiah. This means that Hezekiah's story is recorded three times in the Bible. Once in 2 Kings, again in 2 Chronicles, and last, here in Isaiah chapters 36 through 39. They give us some nice insight into the life of King Hezekiah, of what he did right and how he faltered.

If someone recorded our life story, would we be happy with what they wrote?

[Discover more about King Hezekiah in 2 Kings 18–20 and 2 Chronicles 29–32.]

Day 26:

Prayer Makes a Difference

Isaiah 38

"Go and tell Hezekiah, 'This is what the Lord, the God of your father David, says: I have heard your prayer and seen your tears; I will add fifteen years to your life.'" Isaiah 38:5

Hezekiah puts his confidence in God to *rescue* him from his enemy. God comes through and wipes out the Assyrian army. Hezekiah and his troops don't need to do a thing—except trust God. Jerusalem is no longer under siege, and the nation of Judah is free from foreign occupation. Life is good . . . for a while.

But then Hezekiah falls deathly ill. God dispatches Isaiah to tell Hezekiah the bad news: the illness is fatal. "Put your affairs in order," Isaiah says, "because you're going to die."

But Hezekiah doesn't do as Isaiah instructs. Instead, Hezekiah puts his confidence in God to *heal* him from his illness. He prays for more time. Hezekiah doesn't give God a kind, heartfelt, or even respectful, "Thanks for the heads-up." Rather, the king cries bitter tears and reminds God—as if God needed reminding—of his lifetime of faithfulness, devotion, and right living.

Guess what happens next? God hears Hezekiah's prayers and sees his tears. God comes up with a new plan. Yep. He changes his mind. Instead of sticking to plan A, that the king's end is near, God makes plan B. He sends Isaiah to deliver the good news, and God heals Hezekiah of his fatal ailment.

To offer proof of God's power to do as he promised, he makes the sun move backward for a while. That's convincing: shadows retreat rather than advance. Then everything returns to normal, the sun again moves forward.

Hezekiah lives another fifteen years. This allows him to continue to serve his Lord and rule the people.

But this isn't the first time God changes his mind. Several centuries earlier, he also relented from what he had planned. It was Moses asking God for a different outcome that time.

By seeking God through sincere prayer, Hezekiah and Moses cause God to change his mind.

Do we think we can change God's mind when we seek him?

[Discover other times when God changed his mind in Exodus 32:9–14 and 1 Kings 21:29, as well as a time when he didn't: Mark 14:32–36 and Luke 22:42–44.]

Day 27:

Don't Show Off

Isaiah 39–40

The prophet asked, "What did they see in your palace?" "They saw everything in my palace," Hezekiah said. "There is nothing among my treasures that I did not show them." Isaiah 39:4

First, Hezekiah earnestly seeks God, and God rescues him. Then Hezekiah earnestly seeks God, and God heals him. Our God saves *and* heals—he did that for Hezekiah, and he can do it for us.

Now, having peace and health, everything is going good for King Hezekiah, right? Not so.

The king of Babylon hears that King Hezekiah was on his deathbed and then recovered. The Babylonian king dispatches his envoys with letters and a gift.

Hezekiah receives the men, the king's letters, and the gift. But instead of making the wise move to treat the visitors with caution as potential foreign adversaries, Hezekiah welcomes them as friends, taking them on a grand tour of his palace and his kingdom. Out of pride, he shows them his great wealth. Bad move. Now his enemy knows how much treasure exists in the kingdom of Judah.

God is not pleased and pronounces judgment quickly. Isaiah delivers the message with harsh words to King Hezekiah, chastising him for showing the envoys everything. The king's pride caused him to impress his visitors by showing off his great wealth.

"The time is coming, King Hezekiah, when Babylon will cart off everything you showed them," the prophet says. "They'll leave nothing."

Though it won't happen for another hundred years, Babylon does attack Judah and haul off all its wealth, along with forcibly relocating most of its people. The king of Babylon will capture, castrate, and cart off some of Hezekiah's descendants, forcing them to serve the Babylonian Empire.

We're left to wonder what might have happened if Hezekiah had not pridefully shown off all his wealth. Is it possible that Babylon would not have attacked, conquered, and pillaged Judah a century later?

But this warning is for the future and doesn't directly impact Hezekiah. It affects his descendants. And since he'll avoid unpleasantness, he accepts God's punishment, selfishly glad that he will enjoy peace and security during his lifetime. He doesn't care what happens to his family line.

This leaves us with a second thing to ponder. Hezekiah put his confidence in God to save Jerusalem and the nation. God came through. Next Hezekiah sought God for healing from his fatal illness. God came through. With this history of trusting God and receiving blessings, why doesn't King Hezekiah seek God for a different outcome this time? The king could have boldly sought God instead of passively accepting what he said.

Regardless, Hezekiah's foolish actions and pride bring him and his family to this place.

When has our pride caused us problems?

[Discover more about pride in Leviticus 26:18–20, 2 Chronicles 26:16, 2 Chronicles 32:24–31, Psalm 10:4, Proverbs 16:18, James 1:9–10, and 1 John 2:16.]

Dig Deeper:

Gentiles

"I will keep you and will make you to be a covenant for the people and a light for the Gentiles." Isaiah 42:6

In the Bible, the Hebrews view the world as containing two people groups. One is the Jews—themselves. And they consider everyone else a Gentile.

As God's chosen people, the Jews see themselves as special. They are God's selected nation, his favorite people. Spiritually, they feel they're better than the Gentiles. We get this perspective if we skim the Old Testament. But if we read with care, we see that God also has a heart for Gentiles. We find this truth embedded in many of the prophecies, especially Isaiah's.

Though Isaiah uses *Gentiles* only twice, he refers to them generically as *the people* (forty-four times), *the nations* (thirty-nine times), *all nations* (seven times), and *all people* (five times). Jesus comes for the Jews *and* the Gentiles: everyone. Just as those about God's chosen people, many of the prophecies about the Gentiles carry criticism and condemnation, but others emerge full of hope and promise.

Through Jesus, there is justice not just for the Jews but the Gentiles too. Jesus rescues and saves everyone.

Jesus came to save all people, but do our attitudes and actions prove that we really believe this?

[Discover more of Isaiah's inclusive prophecies in Isaiah 2:2, Isaiah 11:10, Isaiah 14:26, Isaiah 41:1, Isaiah 43:9, Isaiah 49:22, Isaiah 51:4–5, Isaiah 56:7, and Isaiah 66:18–20.]

Day 28:

Jesus and Justice

Isaiah 41–42

"Here is my servant, whom I uphold, my chosen one in whom I delight; I will put my Spirit on him, and he will bring justice to the nations." Isaiah 42:1

After giving us four chapters of historical narrative, Isaiah shifts back to more prophecy. His future-focused look tells us about Jesus. Though Jesus is God's Son, as our Savior—the Messiah—he is also God's servant, who will come to earth in service of Father God to restore us into a right relationship with him. God chose Jesus to redeem his people, for God delights in him.

Under the power of God's Spirit, the Messiah will champion justice. This justice isn't only for the nation of Judah, but it's for all nations—all people, everyone.

This Savior will not proclaim his message with loud, boisterous words but with gentleness. He will protect the weak and encourage those who struggle.

Jesus will faithfully promote justice, never wavering from his mission. Through his followers, both then and now, he will persist until he spreads justice throughout the entire world.

Centuries after Isaiah's prophecy, when Jesus comes to earth, he will come to heal and to save. Today most people seek Jesus for his saving power, while two thousand years ago people came to him more for his healing power.

Where does justice fit into all this?

The people in the Old Testament expected that the promised Savior would come as a military leader to rescue them from their oppressors. They assumed he would be an actual king, in the line of King David, ushering in an era of justice. They believed that at his arrival, the Jews would finally receive fair treatment meted out by a morally righteous leader. He would be true in all he does, governing his people with excellence and protecting them from the immoral oppression of ungodly leaders from opposing nations.

Most of us don't see Jesus today as a physical Savior but as a spiritual Savior. However, throughout the world, many people struggle under the weight of oppressive regimes. They need physical deliverance. They seek the Savior who will provide them with justice. They need Jesus.

We all do.

Do we view Jesus as our savior, healer, or provider of justice? Can he be all three?

[Discover more about justice in Psalm 89:14, Proverbs 16:10, Jeremiah 21:11–12, Matthew 12:17–21, Matthew 23:23, Luke 18:3–8, Hebrews 1:8–9, and Revelation 19:11.]

Dig Deeper:

Names Matter

*"Bring my sons from afar and my daughters
from the ends of the earth—everyone who
is called by my name, whom I created
for my glory, whom I formed and made."*
Isaiah 43:6–7

Isaiah gives several names for God. We call him *Wonderful Counselor*, *Mighty God*, *Everlasting Father*, and *Prince of Peace*. (See Day 5: "A Child Is Born".) His name is the *Lord Almighty*, our *Maker*, the *Holy One*, *Redeemer*, and *God of All the Earth*. Furthermore, he also bears the names *Repairer of Broken Walls* and *Restorer of Streets with Dwellings*.

That's a lot of names. When we merge them together, it gives us a great image of God's character, power, and salvation.

Isaiah also gives some names for Jerusalem (Zion), which can metaphorically apply to us. No longer will the names *Deserted* and *Desolate* apply. In their place will be the names of *My Delight Is in Her* (Hephzibah) and *Married* (Beulah). Then come new names: *Holy People*, the *Redeemed of the Lord*, *Sought After*, the *City No Longer Deserted*, the *City of Righteousness*, and the *Faithful City*. And the name of the road to get there is the *Way of Holiness*.

But most important, God will rescue everyone called by his name.

What name do we use for God? What name does he use for us?

[Discover more about names for God in Isaiah 9:6, Isaiah 54:5, Isaiah 58:12, and Isaiah 62:4. Read about names for Jerusalem (and us) in Isaiah 1:26, Isaiah 4:3, Isaiah 62:4, and Isaiah 62:12.]

Day 29:

I Am

Isaiah 43–44

"This is what the Lord says—Israel's King and Redeemer, the Lord Almighty: I am the first and I am the last; apart from me there is no God." Isaiah 44:6

The people of Judah have a struggle. And it is not unique to them. Throughout their history, God's people have vacillated between two perspectives: pursuing the Lord as their God and pursuing idols. We know which one is right: pursuing God. But through too much of their history, God's people turned their backs on their Lord and worshiped idols.

Now, as if to underscore the importance of pursuing God, he reminds them of who he is. In this regard, Isaiah quotes what the Lord says.

For starters, he is Israel's King. We may think of Saul as Israel's first king. From a historical perspective, he is. Or we may think of David, Israel's second king, who was a man after God's own heart. But before David and before Saul, Israel had no human king. God was their King. They had the ultimate theocracy.

Next, he is our Redeemer. To redeem something is to pay off its debt, to set it free, to atone for it. Jesus—who is God—is our Redeemer. He sacrificed himself for us—for you and me—to pay off our debt of sin, to set us free from its burden, and to make amends for our mistakes. In Jesus and through Jesus, we're redeemed and made right with Father God.

Third, he is Almighty. As the Almighty, he is sovereign and supreme. Omnipotent, he is all-powerful, exercising absolute power. As such, he takes second place to no one.

Fourth, he is the first and the last. He is the beginning and the end, the Alpha and the Omega. The Lord was present at creation, and he will emerge as central in the end times when he turns what is into what will be: a new heaven and a new earth.

Last, he alone is God. No one else can make that claim. Without him we have lost our way—eternally so.

Oh, and there's one more thing.

When the Lord talks about being the first and last, he uses the phrase *I Am*. This may mean nothing to us today, but it meant a lot to the people back then. When Moses encountered God at the burning bush, God tells Moses to identify him as *I Am*. And several millennia later when the mob came to arrest Jesus, he implies that he is *I Am*. The mob pulls back in shock. They should.

The Lord is our King, our Redeemer, our almighty Lord, our eternal God, and the great *I Am*.

Is this how we perceive the Lord God? What do we need to change in our perspective of who God is?

[Discover more about God being the first and the last in Isaiah 48:12, Revelation 1:17, Revelation 2:8, and Revelation 22:13. Learn more about the great *I Am* in Exodus 3:11–15, Mark 12:26, and John 18:4–6.]

Dig Deeper:

There Is No Other

"Then you will know that I am in Israel, that I am the Lord your God, and that there is no other; never again will my people be shamed."
Joel 2:27

Another phrase recurs three times in Isaiah. God says, "I am the Lord, and there is no other." He also phrases it as, "I am God, and there is no other." This wording occurs in only four verses in Isaiah and once in Joel.

However, breaking this phrase into two parts reveals many more occurrences. The first part, "I am the Lord" occurs 155 times in the Bible, all but once in the Old Testament. And the alternate wording "I am God" comes up ten more times.

The second part, "there is no other," appears thirteen times in the Bible. We worship and serve the Lord God, and there is no other like him. He is without equal and stands above all other pursuits. He alone is worthy of our complete devotion and love.

There is no other who can save us.

Do we truly believe that God is our Lord and there is no other?

[Discover more about this phrase in Isaiah 45:5–6, Isaiah 45:18, Isaiah 45:22, and Isaiah 46:9, as well as Mark 12:32 and Acts 4:12.]

Day 30:

Fate or Freedom?

Isaiah 45–46

"I make known the end from the beginning, from ancient times, what is still to come."
Isaiah 46:10

Isaiah, quoting God's own words, says that God knows how things will end before they began. That is, he understands what will happen in the future. And he knew all this before he created us and our world. What he says will occur. And what he plans will happen.

This passage in the Bible—and others like it—makes some people squirm. While many people find comfort in knowing that God is in control, not everyone feels this way. For them, this concept causes consternation because they wonder if we can truly choose our own path and direct our future. We want God to be in control—except for when we don't.

Two big theological concepts emerge from this dilemma: predestination and free will. Since they seem mutually exclusive, a theological conundrum results concerning free will versus predestination.

Hold on. Don't bail on me.

Many people get all worked up about this subject, but I don't want you to be one of them. While the Bible teaches that we can make our own choices (free will), it also says that what happens is predetermined (predestined).

Which is it? Both.

Embracing the concept that predestination and free will can happily coexist presents us with a delightful paradox. Yes, I delight in spiritual paradoxes. Though my mind can grasp predestination and free will as a holistic, unified truth, I woefully struggle to explain it.

It helps a little to consider that we can understand "predestined" to mean "foreknew." This gives some clarity, but it still falls short.

Another helpful consideration is to realize that God—who created time-space—exists outside of his creation. He views time from afar, seeing the past, present, and future as a single reality, whereas we view past, present, and future as three segments of our existence. We experience time as a progression, while God stands outside of time and views it as a unified actuality. He knows what we will choose to do in the future because to him it has already occurred.

Consider the book of Daniel. He prophesies about evil King Nebuchadnezzar. Because of Nebuchadnezzar's prideful arrogance, insanity will strike him until he acknowledges God (free will), and it will take seven years for him to do so (predestination).

Free will and predestination are not mutually exclusive concepts but opposite sides of the same reality. May we thank God for both, while acknowledging that we might never fully grasp how they interconnect.

Do we marvel at God for spiritual paradoxes or get mad about things we can't yet understand?

[Discover more about predestination and free will in Genesis 2:16–17, Proverbs 16:9, Daniel 4:24–25, Romans 8:29, and Revelation 3:20.]

Dig Deeper:

Who Is Bel?

"Bel bows down, Nebo stoops low; their idols are borne by beasts of burden. The images that are carried about are burdensome, a burden for the weary." Isaiah 46:1

In his prophecy, Isaiah makes a brief mention of Bel. He says Bel will bow down. The implication is that Bel is an idol, one of Babylon's gods. The Bible mentions Bel only two other times, both in the book of Jeremiah. Jeremiah also predicts shame and punishment for Bel—and implicitly the Babylonians, who worship him.

That's all the Bible tells us about Bel. Or is it?

The Apocrypha (scriptural text not included in all Bibles) has an extraordinary story about Daniel confronting Bel. When pressured to worship Bel, Daniel claims that Bel is a mere idol made by human hands and not a god who can do anything or is worthy of worship. And Daniel proves it. As a result, Bel's priests and their families are executed, and Daniel destroys the idol of Bel and the temple that housed it.

Though we don't worship an actual idol like Bel, what do we worship instead of God?

[Discover more about Bel in Jeremiah 50:2 and Jeremiah 51:44. Read about the showdown between Daniel and Bel in Daniel 14:1–22 in The New Jerusalem Bible, Common English Bible (CEB), New American Bible (NAB), and other translations. Though this is usually Daniel 14, some versions have this story as a separate, one-chapter book called Bel and the Dragon.]

Day 31:

Our Mentor

Isaiah 47–48

"I am the Lord your God, who teaches you what is best for you, who directs you in the way you should go." Isaiah 48:17

Do you ever wish you had a mentor? We can have mentors in school, mentors at work, and mentors for life. A school mentor can help us get the most from our education. A work mentor can help us advance our careers and find increased vocational success. And a life mentor can help us get the most out of our time here on earth and maximize our impact on others.

Our most important mentor, however, is a spiritual mentor. I have enjoyed times in my life when another person walked alongside me as a spiritual guide. They mentored me in my walk with Jesus.

Their impact on me continued even after our circumstances changed and we could no longer hang out.

Do you desire to have a spiritual mentor? I do. I most certainly do.

We typically think of a mentor as being another person we meet with, but it doesn't have to be that way. A person can mentor us from afar, such as through books. In this regard, the Bible can mentor us. Even more so, God can mentor us through his Holy Spirit.

Aside from the Bible and the Holy Spirit mentoring us, we must make sure the mentors we select are qualified to guide us. If we make our mentor selection poorly, we could end up with the situation Jesus warned about, with one blind person trying to lead another. They will fall into a hole together.

When Isaiah reminds us of the option of God being a spiritual mentor, he starts by giving us God's credentials. He is our Lord, our Lord God. He is our Redeemer, who saves us. And he is holy. No one can be more credentialed as a spiritual mentor than that.

As our mentor, God—through the Bible and Holy Spirit—teaches us life's best practices. He directs us in right living, what the Bible calls righteousness. Furthermore, God guides us in where to go. He lights our paths and directs our journeys.

Unfortunately, after Isaiah tells us about God's qualifications as a mentor and what he can accomplish, we learn that God's people are bad followers. They didn't pay attention to what he said. They ignored his advice. If they had listened to him, they would have enjoyed peace, well-being, and a family legacy. But God's people rejected him as their mentor. They thought they could do better on their own. They were wrong.

If you can find a person who will mentor you spiritually, embrace them as a God-given provision. But whether we have a human mentor or not, remember that God is our ultimate spiritual Mentor who guides us through his Word and his Spirit.

How well do we do at embracing God as our spiritual mentor? Is there anyone we can mentor?

[Discover more about having a spiritual mentor in Exodus 4:12, Luke 6:39–40, Luke 12:11–12, and John 14:26.]

Dig Deeper:

Peace Like a River

"If only you had paid attention to my commands, your peace would have been like a river." Isaiah 48:18

Isaiah talks a lot about peace, mentioning it more than any other book in Scripture. One-tenth of the Bible's references to peace occur in this one book. That's a lot of peace in one place. And God is the source of this peace.

Isaiah's most notable mention about peace concerns Jesus, declaring that he will be the Prince of Peace. His rule and peace will last forever.

Most of Isaiah's passages about peace look forward to a time of future peacefulness. He talks about resting in peace, enjoying perfect peace, and living in peace. God calls his people to make peace with him. And he promises that peace will be the outcome of righteous living. Death for God's people will usher us into eternal peace.

God will create peace for his people. And we are to proclaim peace as we promote the good news of God's salvation. It's a beautiful thing.

An oft-quoted one-liner about peace is God saying, "There's no peace for the wicked." Isaiah writes this in two places, so we'd better not miss it.

And last, but significant, are two verses about peace like a river, which inspired a classic hymn "It Is Well with My Soul" (sometimes called "When Peace Like a River"). It praises God for the awesome peace he provides. And let's not forget about the more contemporary chorus, "I've Got Peace like a River."

We can find true peace from God here on earth now, and after that we'll enjoy peace with him forever.

Do we enjoy peace like a river? If not, what are we missing?

[Discover more about peace in 1 Kings 4:24, Isaiah 9:6–7, Isaiah 48:22, Isaiah 52:7, Isaiah 57:21, Isaiah 66:12, John 14:27, and Galatians 5:22–23.]

Day 32:

A Light to the World

Isaiah 49–50

"I will also make you a light for the Gentiles, that my salvation may reach to the ends of the earth." Isaiah 49:6

The phrases *God's people, the chosen ones, the chosen*, and other similar references appear in multiple places throughout the Old Testament. This designation certainly makes the Jewish people feel special. After all, God chose them to be *his* people. This must mean he likes them better than everyone else. Or to extend this thought a bit further, it must mean he doesn't like any of the other nations as much.

It's easy for God's people to assume that he loves them and hates everyone else. Therefore, when God's prophets tell of rescue, salvation, and favor, the

Hebrew people (the Jews) surely assume he directs his words to them, his chosen ones. They are in, and everyone else is out.

A quick reading of the Old Testament supports this exclusive perspective. But if we slow down and read carefully, we see that God has a different point of view. Yes, he wants a relationship with his chosen people, the Jews. But he also wants a relationship with everyone else, all nations and all people, regardless of their ethnicity or country of origin. God is inclusive. Never forget that.

We first get a glimpse of this in Genesis. God says he will bless Abraham and through him God will, in turn, bless all nations. What will this blessing through Abraham look like? We could interpret this as material blessing—and there is some argument for that—but a more enlightened understanding is that God wants to spiritually bless *everyone* through Abraham. Jesus, a direct descendant of Abraham, accomplishes this by dying to make all people right with Father God.

We find this salvation for all nations repeated throughout the Old Testament. The Psalms mention it, along with several of the prophets: Jeremiah,

Daniel, Joel, Obadiah, and Haggai. But Isaiah leads them all in reminding God's chosen people that he wants to save everyone, not just the Jews. This means Gentiles too. The Jews—through Jesus—will be a light to the Gentiles. I'm so glad to hear this because I'm a Gentile. I suspect you are too.

Jesus comes for everyone: all nations, all people—the Gentiles. And to make sure we don't miss this, John's epic revelation about the end times confirms that all nations will come to God and worship him.

Do we ever think that God favors us, and we deserve his salvation more than others?

[Discover more about God saving all people and all nations in Genesis 18:18, Psalm 67:1–5, Isaiah 2:2, Jeremiah 3:17, Daniel 7:14, Haggai 2:7, and Revelation 15:4.]

Day 33:

Bring Good News

Isaiah 51–52

How beautiful on the mountains are the feet of those who bring good news. Isaiah 52:7

Isaiah's prophetic words look forward to the future. His prophecies often carry a double meaning, looking at a tangible fulfillment in the near term and a spiritual fulfillment later. Today's passage is one such example. It may even carry a triple application: short-term, long-term, and intermediate.

In the short-term, Isaiah predicts the people exiled in Babylon will return home to Judah. This good news is of peace and repatriation—that is, their physical salvation. They will praise God for his deliverance.

For the long-term, in the future we still anticipate, Isaiah looks forward to Jesus's return to earth, not his first coming, which was two thousand years ago, but his second coming, which we still anticipate. Then he will rule from Jerusalem, that is, the mountain of Zion. This, too, is good news of peace, good tidings, and salvation. And for this, we will celebrate the reign of Jesus.

Last, Paul, in his letter to the church in Rome, gives us a third understanding of this future-focused passage. This is the aspect that resonates most with us today. It celebrates telling people about Jesus and their believing in that message to receive their salvation.

Paul starts the discussion by quoting this verse from Isaiah. But then he points out that not all Jews accepted Isaiah's message of good news—not then and not in Paul's day either. He Paul reminds us that faith comes from hearing. And though others did their part to share the gospel—with the Jews as well as the entire world—not everyone chose to listen.

The Jews did not understand. But the Gentiles who weren't seeking Jesus heard about him instead. God revealed his Son to those who hadn't asked for help. Still, God has a heart for his chosen people. He wants them to come to him and receive the salvation he offers.

Paul wraps up his teaching by quoting another passage from Isaiah. Here God says that he holds out his hands to his people, waiting for them to come to him. He remains vigilant all day long. He does this even though they disobey him and are obstinate. He is patient, and his love doesn't waver, even for those who don't respond.

How comforting to know that God loves us and is patient. We can count on it. We need to, because sometimes we're the ones who are disobedient and obstinate. And for his patient love, we can praise God.

Have we accepted Jesus's good news? Are we telling others about it so they may hear?

[Discover more about good news in Isaiah 40:9, Isaiah 41:27, Nahum 1:15, and Romans 10:14–16.]

Dig Deeper:

The Arm of the Lord

Who has believed our message and to whom has the arm of the Lord been revealed?
Isaiah 53:1

The phrase *the arm of the Lord* appears four times in the Bible. Isaiah uses it three times and John quotes Isaiah for the fourth appearance. Isaiah also mentions God's arm sixteen times, more times than any other book in the Bible. Jeremiah, Ezekiel, and Zechariah also mention God's arm.

We can understand God's arm as exemplifying his strength. It's a metaphor for power, his all-encompassing power to do anything he wants. We call this omnipotence, which means "all-powerful."

Because of God's strong arm, he can deliver people under oppression. His people long for deliverance.

That's why the prophets mention God's strong arm so often.

Though the long arm of the Lord is strong enough to deliver the people clamoring for rescue at any time, he often delays. We can debate why he forestalls action, ranging from accusations of apathy to questioning how much power he has. In truth, we'll never know for sure until we get to heaven and ask him. For now, we should accept that his reasons are just, and his timing is perfect. This requires faith, and faith is what we need when we follow him.

How do we react when we don't understand God's ways or like his timing?

[Discover more about the arm of the Lord in Isaiah 51:9, Isaiah 59:1, and John 12:38, as well as Exodus 6:6, Numbers 11:23, Job 40:9, Psalm 89:13, Isaiah 50:2, Jeremiah 21:5, Ezekiel 20:33, and Luke 1:51.]

Day 34:

Sing and Rejoice

Isaiah 53–54

"Sing, barren woman, you who never bore a child; burst into song, shout for joy, you who were never in labor; because more are the children of the desolate woman than of her who has a husband," says the Lord.
Isaiah 54:1

In today's passage, Isaiah shares some shocking words from God. He tells childless women to sing, for a song to erupt from them in a burst of joy. How strange. Children are an important part of the culture in Isaiah's day. The practical application is having children who could work in the family business—usually agrarian, tending crops and caring for animals. Of imperative nature to the moms, however, is that they live in a patriarchal society. (This isn't

God's plan but man's doing.) Therefore, having children to care for them should they become a widow—which is highly likely—is critical to their survival.

The Bible has many accounts of women who want to be moms but wait years in hopeful desperation. Consider Sarah, who doesn't give birth to her only child, Isaac, until she's ninety.

Two generations later, Rachel remains childless while her husband fathers children with her maid, her sister, and her sister's maid. (Yeah, it's messed up.) At last Rachel gives birth to Joseph and later Benjamin, Jacob's two youngest boys.

Or consider Hannah, who remains childless while her co-wife Peninnah (another messed-up situation) has several children. In passionate prayer she begs God for a son, promising to dedicate him to a lifetime of service to God. A year later, Samuel is born.

In the New Testament we learn that Elizabeth and her husband, Zechariah, trust God for a child well into their old age. Eventually she gives birth to John, whom we know as John the Baptist.

God comes through for each one of these women, along with many others, by blessing them with children. So why then would God tell childless women to shout songs of joy? Could this foreshadow the words of Jesus when he tells the women not to cry for him as he nears his crucifixion? "There will come a time," he says, "when it will be a blessing to be childless," anticipating a future day when people will flee for their lives.

No, it's not that either.

God is telling childless women to celebrate for what he *will* do for them. He will bless them with children, so many that their tents won't be large enough. They'll need bigger tents to accommodate their growing families. Eventually, the Jews' numbers will increase so much that they'll spread out to dispose other nations and settle there. Now that's something to sing about.

What can we praise God for in jubilant songs that we shout with joy?

[Discover more about God's provision for childless women in Genesis 17:17–19, Genesis 21:1–7, Genesis 30:1–24, 1 Samuel 1:1–20, Luke 1:5–25, and Luke 1:57–66. Also see Luke 23:28–29.]

Day 35:

Seek God

Isaiah 55–56

Seek the Lord while he may be found; call on him while he is near. Isaiah 55:6

Isaiah warns the people to seek God. The prophet advises them to do so before it's too late, while they still have a chance to find him. They should call to him when he is close by. It's an imperative invitation to evil people—that is, sinners—to make a U-turn from their wrong actions and thoughts, aligning themselves with God and his ways. When they do so, God will mercifully pardon them. He will do so at no cost to them.

This makes it sound like the opportunity to follow God is a limited-time offer. We had better grab it now before it's too late. Act now before God discontinues the product or the sale ends. That's not it at all. God's gift of salvation stands forever. He never withdraws his offer, never changes the terms and conditions, and never adjusts the price—free.

The urgency is from our perspective. We don't know what tomorrow will hold. We don't even know about the next second. Our lives could end at any moment. That's why we should act now.

Centuries later Jesus teaches this lesson in one of his parables. He tells of a rich man whose crops produced an abundant yield, a great harvest. But he has no place to store the bounty God blessed him with. The man comes up with a plan. He decides to tear down his storage buildings and build bigger ones, large enough to store the great harvest. Then he can sit back and coast for many years, taking life easy with food, drink, and merriment.

God is not impressed.

The foolish man will die that night. His plans will mean nothing. Someone else will enjoy what he tried to stockpile for himself. So it will be when our priorities are off. We shouldn't amass things for ourselves. Instead, we should seek God's riches. We should do so while it is still today because we don't know what will happen tomorrow. Only God does.

Another time Jesus gives two more short parables to make his point. One is the parable of a hidden treasure, and the other is the parable of a valuable pearl. Both have the same lesson: don't let anything get in the way of pursuing God, the most valuable of all pursuits.

Still another time Jesus says to seek God first. Then all other concerns will fall into place. Psalms and Proverbs concur. So does the writer of Hebrews.

When we seek to put God first, he will then reward us with other things.

What do we do to seek God and give him first place in our lives?

[Discover more about seeking God in Deuteronomy 4:29, Psalm 14:2, Psalm 27:4, Psalm 63:1, Matthew 6:33, Romans 3:10–11, and Hebrews 11:6. Also read three of Jesus's parables about seeking God in Matthew 13:44–46 and Luke 12:16–21.]

Day 36:

Fasting, Failure, and Fisticuffs

Isaiah 57–58

"Yet on the day of your fasting, you do as you please and exploit all your workers. Your fasting ends in quarreling and strife, and in striking each other with wicked fists. You cannot fast as you do today and expect your voice to be heard on high." Isaiah 58:3–4

To fast means to go without food. Though I'm still looking, I haven't found any place in the Bible that commands us to fast. I was sure I'd find a reference to it in the Law of Moses, but it's not there. In fact, the first time the Bible mentions fasting is centuries later in Judges. There it simply mentions that the Israelite army fasts in sorrow after 18,000 soldiers die in a civil war. No one tells them to fast. No one encourages them to fast. They just do it. It seems fasting has already become a spiritual practice by this time.

The Old Testament describes instances of people fasting thirty-one times. Yet fasting is not just an Old Testament tradition. The New Testament mentions fasting twenty more times. Jesus fasts for forty days before he begins his ministry, but he never tells his disciples to fast, and they never do. Even so, the practice of fasting continues with the early church in Acts, but Acts is the last book in the New Testament to mention fasting.

Fasting is a spiritual discipline. The idea of fasting has also expanded to include withholding other things in our lives besides food. The practice to give up something for Lent is a form of fasting.

The closest thing we have to a biblical command to fast comes from the lips of Jesus. He begins teaching about fasting with the phrase, "When you fast . . ." Notice he doesn't say *if*. He says *when*. He expects his followers will fast. Then he gives some instructions about the practice.

As you might expect, Isaiah has something to say about fasting too. Actually, it's God's words, which Isaiah records. It's a warning. This is because the people do it wrong. Yes, they go through the motions of not eating, but their hearts are elsewhere. They do as they please when they fast. For example, they oppress their employees. And by the time their fast wraps up, they're arguing and causing conflict. This evolves into a fistfight. Yep, fasting fisticuffs. So when these people fast, they abuse their workers, argue, and fight.

This isn't what God wants. He wants fasting that produces humility. Beyond that, he wants *fasting* that battles injustice and frees the oppressed. Our fasting—going without food—should be the occasion to share food with those who are hungry. Our fasting should also provide shelter and clothing to those in need.

When we fast in this way we'll serve as a witness, receive our healing, and have right living lead us into peace and prosperity.

If all this seems strange or confusing, remember that it's God's own words, which Isaiah wrote down for us to read. So don't breeze through this passage. Instead, carefully consider what God desires.

Do we practice the spiritual discipline of fasting? How should we change our practice of fasting?

[Discover more about fasting in Judges 20:26, Matthew 6:16–18, Luke 4:1–2, Luke 5:33, Acts 13:2–3, and Acts 14:23.]

Day 37:

No More Sun

Isaiah 59–60

"The sun will no more be your light by day, nor will the brightness of the moon shine on you, for the Lord will be your everlasting light, and your God will be your glory."
Isaiah 60:19

I relish sunshine. I suspect most people who don't live in sweltering areas do too. Cloudy days discourage me, even though the rain they may produce is essential. But sunny days are the best.

However, Isaiah looks to a future when we won't need the sun to light our day or even the moon to help us see at night. The glory of the Lord God will provide us with all the light we need, forever and ever. The Son of God will replace the sun in the sky. How awesome is that?

In this future, there's no need for the sun to shine or the moon to glow. The brilliance of God will provide all the light we need. God will be our everlasting light. His supernatural glow will surround us with the light of his splendor.

Now let's jump forward to another prophetic book—the only one in the New Testament—Revelation. The all-out battle to end all battles in John's epic revelation continues. Just before Babylon—the symbol of all that's evil—is about to receive her final punishment, an angel comes from heaven.

John writes that this angel has great authority, and his splendor illuminates the earth. I don't know if this angel's great authority makes him an archangel or not, but it does make him quite special. This may be why he shines so brightly. Of course, remember that he's been in God's presence. Beings who spend time in God's company tend to glow. This happened to Moses several millennia earlier.

Imagine that. An angel who shines bright enough to light up the whole earth. This isn't a searchlight that illuminates one spot at a time, but a floodlight that lights up everything.

But this angel isn't the only one who shines brightly. This is only a hint of what is to come. Later in Revelation, John writes that in the future—in the new heaven and new earth—there will be no need to light a lamp or for the sun to shine. This is because the glory of the Lord God will be our light, the only light we'll need. Night is gone. No more darkness. Only light. And this light comes from God.

When we think of an angel lighting up the world by the glory of his authority, that's an amazing image. Though I doubt he'll radiate as much as the sun, I do know that in our future home, God's splendor will shine so brightly that we won't need the sun to see. The light of God will be the only light we need. And that's more than enough.

Does the light of God shine in us? Do our faces glow after we spend time with him?

[Discover more about supernatural light in Revelation 18:1 and Revelation 22:5. Read about the radiance of Moses's face in Exodus 34:29–35.]

Dig Deeper:

The Armor of God

*He put on righteousness as his breastplate,
and the helmet of salvation on his head;
he put on the garments of vengeance and
wrapped himself in zeal as in a cloak.*
Isaiah 59:17

In his letter to the Ephesians, Paul talks about our preparing for spiritual battle, calling us to put on the armor of God. Paul also talks about this in his first letter to the Thessalonian church, and Peter mentions our faith in God's power shielding us as we wait for the revelation of his salvation.

However, we can attribute the basis for this armor of God imagery to Isaiah. He talks about God strapping on his own breastplate of righteousness and helmet of salvation. He, as our Protector, wrapped in a cloak of zeal, will don garments of vengeance. He's prepared to fight for us. It's a powerful image.

Paul, however, calls *us* to wear the full armor of God. Using an image everyone was familiar with at that time, a Roman soldier, Paul taps it as a memory aid to help the people grasp six essential items:

1. Truth, as in the belt of truth
2. Right living, as in the breastplate of righteousness
3. Peace, as in feet fitted with peace through Jesus
4. Faith, as in the shield of faith to protect us from the evil one's assaults
5. Salvation, as in the helmet of salvation
6. God's Spirit, as in the sword of the Spirit, which is the Word of God

As followers of Jesus, may we hold on to truth, right living, peace, faith, salvation, and God's Spirit.

How good are we at "wearing" truth, right living, peace, faith, salvation, and God's Spirit?

[Discover more about the armor of God in Ephesians 6:10–20 and 1 Thessalonians 5:8, as well as 1 Peter 1:3–5.]

Day 38:

Be Like Jesus

Isaiah 61-62

The Spirit of the Sovereign Lord is on me, because the Lord has anointed me to proclaim good news to the poor. He has sent me to bind up the brokenhearted, to proclaim freedom for the captives and release from darkness for the prisoners, to proclaim the year of the Lord's favor and the day of vengeance of our God, to comfort all who mourn, and provide for those who grieve in Zion. Isaiah 61:1-3

Isaiah prophetically tells the people that the coming Savior—who we now know is Jesus—will move in Holy Spirit power. He will

- proclaim good news to the poor,
- bind up the brokenhearted,

- declare freedom for the captives and release from darkness for the prisoners,
- announce the year of the Lord's favor and the day of vengeance of our God,
- comfort all who mourn,
- provide for those who grieve, and
- bestow on them a crown of beauty instead of ashes.

Wow, this is quite an impressive list. There's at least one thing there that will resonate with everyone.

Now let's jump forward several centuries to the New Testament. We can read what Jesus has to say about these prophetic words in Isaiah. Here's how the story unfolds.

On the Sabbath, Jesus goes to the synagogue in his hometown to worship God with family and friends. It's his turn to read Scripture, and the day's reading is from Isaiah.

Jesus stands. The synagogue leader hands him the scroll that contains the words of Isaiah. Jesus unrolls it, almost to the end. He reads the passage that we now know as Isaiah 61:1–2. The people are familiar with these words. They've heard them before, and they're anxious for this prophecy to happen. They hope it will occur in their lifetime. They sure do need a Savior to rescue them, to set the oppressed people free—because they are certainly oppressed.

After Jesus reads the passage, he rolls up the scroll, hands it back to the synagogue leader, and sits down. Everyone looks at him, waiting to hear what he has to say. His message isn't long or elegant. It's succinct but powerful. "Today this prophecy is fulfilled." I'm sure there are some shocked gasps when Jesus says this.

These prophetic words from Isaiah are what Jesus will do. It's a mini job description: under the power of God's Spirit, Jesus will speak truth to those who are seeking, provide help to those in need, and give hope to those who hurt.

As Jesus's followers, we should be like him. We should do what he did. It will take a lifetime to put these things into practice. Therefore, God leaves us on earth after we decide to follow Jesus. Being like Jesus and telling others about him is what we should do with our remaining time here.

If we love Jesus, we need to do what he would do. And just as with Jesus, it begins with the Holy Spirit, and we can start today.

How can we put these things into practice? How can we implement one of these actions to help others?

[Discover more about Jesus's job description in Luke 4:16–21.]

Day 39:

Do Not Grieve the Holy Spirit

Isaiah 63–64

Yet they rebelled and grieved his Holy Spirit. So he turned and became their enemy and he himself fought against them. Isaiah 63:10

After Jesus rises from the dead, but before he returns to heaven, he has a message for his disciples. He tells them to wait in Jerusalem for a gift that Papa will send: the Holy Spirit. In the book of Acts, we see the Holy Spirit arrive in dramatic, undeniable power. He becomes the star of Acts.

Given this, we could easily conclude that the Holy Spirit is a New Testament manifestation of God. That would be wrong. The Holy Spirit is active in the Old Testament too. The word *Spirit* (Spirit with a capital S, refers to God) occurs hundreds of times in the Bible, making a respectable showing in the Old Testament, popping up about eighty times in over half of the books. It is true that the full name *Holy Spirit* occurs primarily in the New Testament—ninety-three times versus only three in the Old Testament. But this doesn't diminish the Holy Spirit's active participation at work in the lives of God's chosen people prior to his official outpouring on Jesus's disciples.

And for the three times when the Old Testament uses the complete name *Holy Spirit*, one occurs in a psalm and the other two in Isaiah.

In the passage in Psalms, remorse seizes David over his adultery with Bathsheba. He begs God for mercy and asks God to cleanse him from his sin. He is a broken man. As David continues in his prayer, he implores God not to take the Holy Spirit from him. That, it seems, would be a punishment too great for him to bear.

The passage in Isaiah mentions the *Holy Spirit* twice and the *Spirit of the Lord* once. The people have rebelled against God and caused his Holy Spirit to grieve. God responded by turning against them. The people can't figure it out. They remember accounts of how the Holy Spirit was with Moses when their ancestors fled Egypt. They recall how Moses—under

Holy Spirit power—separated the waters so the people could escape the Egyptian army. Then the Holy Spirit gave them rest and guided them. Where is the Holy Spirit now? What happened?

The people grieved the Holy Spirit when they rebelled against God.

Paul issues a similar warning to the people in Ephesus not to grieve God's Holy Spirit, who seals their salvation.

Just as a parent grieves over the rebellious actions of a child, so, too, God's Holy Spirit grieves over us if we rebel against him or turn our backs on the salvation we once received.

May we never grieve the Holy Spirit. May he always be in us, guiding us and giving us rest.

How might we grieve the Holy Spirit? What must we change?

[Discover more about the Holy Spirit in Psalm 51:11, Luke 24:49, Acts 1:4, Acts 2:1–12, and Ephesians 4:30.]

Dig Deeper:

The New Heaven and the New Earth

"See, I will create new heavens and a new earth. The former things will not be remembered, nor will they come to mind."
Isaiah 65:17

In Isaiah's prophecy he looks forward to a new heaven and a new earth. He shares some key characteristics of what this new reality will be like.

First, God will create this new heaven and the new earth. When he does, we will not think about the past. In fact, we will not remember it at all. We will not mourn or cry. Pain over what once was will disappear in this new place. We will celebrate with joy what he has made. In this idyllic future, the unspoiled nature of his original creation will return.

Next, the new heaven and new earth will last. We can presume it will endure forever. In the same way, our names will live on. So, too, will our descendants. All people from all nations will come and worship the Lord as their King.

Centuries later, in John's epic revelation, God reinforces these prophetic words. This new heaven and new earth will replace the first heaven and first earth. As the new emerges, the ultimate wedding celebration will occur. In a supernatural union, we—as a beautifully dressed bride—will unite with God. He will live with us and we with him. We will be his people and he will be our God. Death will end. Pain will disappear. And he'll dry our tears. He'll make everything new.

But this doesn't include those who reject Jesus. They'll suffer a second death.

In Peter's second letter, he also anticipates this new heaven and new earth, which God has promised, and we await in expectation. Righteousness will prevail, and we must prepare to join God there.

How should we balance our reality on earth today with God's promise for a new heaven and a new earth?

[Discover more about the new heaven and new earth in Isaiah 65:17–25, Isaiah 66:22–23, 2 Peter 3:11–14, and Revelation 21:1–8.]

Day 40:

Answer the Call

Isaiah 65–66

"I will destine you for the sword, and all of you will fall in the slaughter; for I called but you did not answer, I spoke but you did not listen. You did evil in my sight and chose what displeases me." Isaiah 65:12

Isaiah wraps up his lengthy prophecy talking about judgment. He prophesies that God has destined the people for death. That they will fall, slaughtered.

Why would a loving God want to kill his people?

Through the mouth of Isaiah, God explains. He says that when he calls his people, they don't answer. It would be like you and me passing on a path. You say, "Hi," but I ignore you. That would be rude. It would disrespect you. And that's exactly what God's people do to him. They're rude and disrespectful.

To make sure we don't miss his point, God rephrases his warning. He adds that when he speaks, his people don't listen. This would be like you shouting to me, "Watch out for that car!" But I ignore you, walk into traffic, and bam! A car hits me. So it is with God's people. He tries to warn them, but they don't listen.

Instead of listening, instead of answering, the people do the things God says are evil. They intentionally do what displeases him. They may figure they're free to ignore what God says because they don't think it matters or because they assume there will be no consequences. After all, they haven't seen any for a long time.

However, whether immediate or delayed, their actions will have consequences. So, too, our actions have ramifications. Some happen right away, and others won't occur until later.

At last God's patience with this people is at its breaking point. He says, "Enough is enough. Your time is up. You ignored me and disrespected me long enough. You're about to enter the punishment phase." This is all because they didn't listen to God.

We may have a similar view of God. We may choose to ignore him because we think what he says doesn't matter. We assume we'll still get into heaven regardless of our actions or our inactions. We may conclude there will be no consequences because we haven't seen any yet. However, just because God loves us and will forgive us doesn't mean our wrong actions won't have negative outcomes.

Yet for those who do listen—God's true people—he will take care of them. As God's servants, they will eat, drink, rejoice, and sing. And this goes for us, too, when we listen to God and answer his call.

When God speaks, we better listen. When God calls, we better answer.

Are we listening for God? When he calls, do we answer?

[Discover more about God calling people in Exodus 3:1–4, 1 Samuel 3:1–10, Matthew 4:18–20, Matthew 9:9, Mark 1:16–18, Mark 2:13–14, Luke 5:27–28, John 1:43, and John 21:18–19.]

For Small Groups, Sunday Schools, and Classrooms

For Unto Us makes an ideal eight-week discussion guide for small groups, Sunday schools, and classrooms. In preparation for the conversation, read one chapter of this book each weekday, Monday through Friday.

- Week 1: read 1 through 5.
- Week 2: read 6 through 10.
- Week 3: read 11 through 15.
- Week 4: read 16 through 20.
- Week 5: read 21 through 25.
- Week 6: read 26 through 30.
- Week 7: read 31 through 35.
- Week 8: read 36 through 40.

Then when you get together, discuss the questions at the end of each chapter. The leader can use all the questions to guide your discussion or pick some to focus on.

Before beginning your discussion, pray as a group. Ask for Holy Spirit insight and clarity. While considering each chapter's questions:

- Look for how this can grow your understanding of the Bible.
- Evaluate how this can expand your faith perspective.
- Consider what you need to change in how you live your lives.
- End by asking God to help you apply what you've learned.

May God speak to you as you use this book to study his Word and grow closer to him.

Bonus Content:

If You're New to the Bible

Each entry in this book ends with Bible references. These can guide you if you want to learn more. If you're not familiar with the Bible, here's a brief overview to get you started, give some context, and minimize confusion.

First, the Bible is a collection of works written by various authors over several centuries. Think of the Bible as a diverse anthology of godly communication. It contains historical accounts, poetry, songs, letters of instruction and encouragement, messages from God sent through his representatives, and prophecies.

Most versions of the Bible have sixty-six books grouped into two sections: The Old Testament and the New Testament. The Old Testament contains thirty-nine books that precede and anticipate Jesus. The New Testament includes twenty-seven books and covers Jesus's life and the work of his followers.

The reference notations in the Bible, such as Romans 3:23, are analogous to line numbers in a Shakespearean play. They serve as a study aid. Since the Bible is much longer and more complex than a play, its reference notations are more involved.

As already mentioned, the Bible is an amalgam of books, or sections, such as Genesis, Psalms, John, 1 Peter, or Acts. The names of the books were given to them, over time, based on the piece's author, audience, or purpose.

In the 1200s each book was divided into chapters, such as Acts 2 or Psalm 23. In the 1500s the chapters were further subdivided into verses, such as John 3:16. Let's use this as an example.

The name of the book (John) is first, followed by the chapter number (3), a colon, and then the verse number (16). Sometimes called a chapter-verse reference notation, this helps people quickly locate a specific text regardless of their version of the Bible.

Here's how to locate a specific passage in the Bible based on its reference: Most Bibles contain a table of contents, which gives the page number for the beginning of each book. Start there. Locate the book you want to read, and turn to that page number. Then page forward to find the chapter you want. Last, skim that page to locate the specific verse.

If you want to read online, just pop the entire reference, such as 2 Timothy 3:16, into a search engine, and you'll get lots of links to online resources. You can also go directly to BibleGateway.com or use the YouVersion app.

Although the goal was to place these chapter and verse divisions at logical breaks, they sometimes seem arbitrary. Therefore, it's a good practice to read what precedes and follows each passage we're studying since the text before or after it may contain relevant insight into the portion we're exploring.

Learn more about the greatest book ever written at ABibleADay.com, which provides a Bible blog, summaries of the books of the Bible, a dictionary of Bible terms, Bible reading plans, and other resources.

Acknowledgments

No author works alone. In addition to my team listed in the credits section, I acknowledge essential support from:

My dear friends at Kalamazoo Christian Writers for always pushing me to do better.

My admin, Shara Anjaynith Cazon, for giving me more time to write.

Joanna Penn's podcasts and books for getting me to this point on my author journey.

My ministry team who helps get the word out about my ministry of words.

God: everything starts and ends with you.

And I acknowledge you for reading and considering what I write. May God bless you on your spiritual journey.

About the Dear Theophilus Series

In the Bible, Doctor Luke addresses his books Luke and Acts to Theophilus. We don't know anything about this man. But we do know that Luke writes his books for Theophilus so that he can know for sure what he was taught.

Isn't that the purpose of the whole Bible? So that we may know? In this way, aren't we all like Theophilus?

For Unto Us continues this mission: so that we may know for sure what we've been taught about God. It's part devotional, part Bible study, and part commentary, but it's mostly an exploration of biblical Christianity for today's followers of Jesus.

This is the third book in the Dear Theophilus series. My goal is to cover every book of the Bible. People on my email list will help decide what I'll cover next. Be sure to sign up at peterdehaan.com/email-updates and help pick the topic for the next book in this series.

May this book help you move forward on your spiritual journey.

About Peter DeHaan

Peter DeHaan, PhD, wants to change the world one word at a time. His books and blog posts discuss God, the Bible, and church, geared toward spiritual seekers and church dropouts. Many people feel church has let them down, and Peter seeks to encourage them as they search for a place to belong.

But he's not afraid to ask tough questions or make religious people squirm. He's not trying to be provocative. Instead, he seeks truth, even if it makes people uncomfortable. Peter urges Christians to push past the status quo and reexamine how they practice their faith in every part of their lives.

Peter earned his doctorate, awarded with high distinction, from Trinity College of the Bible and Theological Seminary. He lives with his wife in beautiful Southwest Michigan and wrangles crossword puzzles in his spare time.

Peter's a lifelong student of Scripture. He wrote the 700-page website ABibleADay.com to encourage people to explore the Bible, the greatest book ever written. His popular blog, at PeterDeHaan.com, addresses biblical Christianity to build a faith that matters.

Read his blog, receive his newsletter, and learn more at PeterDeHaan.com.

If you liked *For Unto Us: 40 Prophetic Insights about Jesus, Justice, and Gentiles from the Prophet Isaiah*, please leave a review online. Your review will help others discover this book and encourage them to read it too. That would be amazing.

Thank you.

Books by Peter DeHaan

For the latest list of all Peter's books, go to PeterDeHaan.com/books.

The Dear Theophilus series of devotional Bible studies:
That You May Know (the gospel of Luke)
Tongues of Fire (the book of Acts)
For Unto Us (the prophet Isaiah)
Return to Me (the Minor Prophets)
I Hope in Him (the book of Job)
Living Water (the gospel of John)
Love Is Patient (Paul's letters to the Corinthians)
A New Heaven and a New Earth (John's Revelation)

The 52 Churches series:
52 Churches
The 52 Churches Workbook
More Than 52 Churches
The More Than 52 Churches Workbook
Visiting Online Church

The Bible Bios series:
Women of the Bible
The Friends and Foes of Jesus
Old Testament Sinners and Saints

Other books:
Beyond Psalm 150
Jesus's Broken Church
Bridging the Sacred-Secular Divide
Martin Luther's 95 Theses
How Big Is Your Tent?

Be the first to hear about Peter's new books and receive updates at PeterDeHaan.com/updates.

www.ingramcontent.com/pod-product-compliance
Lightning Source LLC
Chambersburg PA
CBHW072002110526
44592CB00012B/1176